The WorthOf ASoul

The Worth Of A Soul

A PERSONAL ACCOUNT OF EXCOMMUNICATION AND CONVERSION

STEVEN A. CRAMER

ISBN:1-55517-171-0

Published and Distributed by:

CFI
Cedar Fort, Incorporated
925 North Main, Springville, UT 84663 801-489-4084

Cover Design by Lyle Mortimer
Printed in the United States of America
Revised and Reprinted 1995

But thanks be to God, which giveth us
the victory through our Lord Jesus Christ.
(I Cor. 15:57)

To G. P. and C. B. who helped me turn from what I was toward what God wanted me to be . . .

And to my wife and family who stood by me patiently and believed in me through all the years before I turned.

Acknowledgments

I cannot find the words to express my debt and appreciation to my family whose love and patience with me made my conversion possible. I thank them for standing behind me and for believing in me when there was no evidence that I would ever justify their faith. I thank them for granting permission to tell this story. I acknowledge and appreciate the unfailing support of our Bishop as my family struggled to cope with the terrible stress I caused.

I give special thanks to my wife who provided both the courage and the encouragement to relate our experience, and who did all of the endless typing without complaint.

I express gratitude to our friend, D. P., who spent so many hours reviewing the manuscripts and whose editorial comments were invaluable in clarifying the message.

I give my thanks to the publishers of this book for their careful advice and for their courage to bring forth this type of book.

Last of all, I give my thanks to all the excommunicants who shared their hearts and their hurts with me. It was the discovery that their sorrows, problems, and frustrations were so similar to mine that made me know that such a story needed to be told.

The Author

Contents

Prologue

IT IS EARLY in the morning, and I hear a knock on my front door. I have been expecting it. Even so, I open the door apprehensively, for I know what it will mean. There is an awkward silence. I glumly say good morning to my Bishop and the High Priest he has brought with him as a second witness. The mixture of grief and pity which I see in their nervous faces manifests the intense discomfort which they feel. These are my brethren—men with whom I have prayed and served. They hand me an envelope from the Stake President. I already know what it contains: the summons. The summons to a Church court which must be delivered in person by "two trusted Melchizedek Priesthood holders" who can then stand as witnesses that the accused person was properly notified of the action pending. They try to express their sorrow, but soon they turn awkwardly to leave, not knowing what to say.

What can be said at a time such as this when, for one brief moment, all time is frozen? A time when hearts are breaking and all eternity is weeping over the loss of another child of God. Weeping, but not in condemnation or anger, but with the perfect and stubborn love which will not give up even in these unfortunate circumstances.

For a brief moment, as I watch my brethren leave, I feel more sorrow for their pain than for my own. I shut the door and open the letter, already knowing what it will say:

> Dear Brother Cramer,
>
> You are hereby requested to appear before a High Council Court in the High Council room for investigation of your conduct in violation of the law and order of the Church.

The words blur as bitter tears of remorse, confusion, and frustration flood my eyes. With a trembling hand, I wipe the tears away and read the rest of the letter.

> You should be present with witnesses, if you desire them, at the time and place specified. If there is good reason why you cannot be present, please notify the undersigned in due time. In the event of your absence, without excuse, action must necessarily be taken in accordance with the evidence presented and the established procedure of the Church in such matters.

My excommunication process has begun. As I sit there staring at the unbelievable words, I have absolutely no conception of the horrible struggle that lies ahead. But Satan knows what is coming, and somewhere nearby he and his diabolical followers are rejoicing. Satan is about to receive another victim of his deceiving lies. After twenty-eight years of struggle to gain my soul, at last he is going to have me fully within the grasp of his evil power. He has won. I am lost. I am about to be expelled from the Church and Kingdom of God—the Church which I have loved and spent thousands of hours serving. The Church which I have deliberately polluted by my sin. The Church which is now required by the laws of God to expel one who has deliberately violated sacred covenants.

Yes, Satan is rejoicing, certain that he has won. But Satan is wrong. His victory is only temporary. It is true that he now has me wrapped securely in the chains of hell. But the Lord is already planning my rescue! The time will come when I will be delivered by the majesty and power of God's redeeming love. Before this horrible experience is over, both Satan and I are going to learn that it is never "too late." We will learn that absolutely no one who will respond is beyond the reach of the Lord's perfect and unwavering love. The time will come when I will understand that the heights of our joy are proportionate to the depths of our sorrow. Somewhere in the Heavenly Courts above, the beautiful words of the Savior to His grieving Apostles are echoing again:

> Ye shall weep and lament . . . and ye shall be sorrowful, but your sorrow shall be turned into joy. (John 16:20.)

As I finish the letter, the tears flow. How little do I realize that the anguish and torment which I now feel, and that I have caused, and will yet cause, in the hearts of my loved ones has scarcely begun.

I
Suicide

A NUMBER OF years ago I observed the shattering effects of a man's downfall. One of my fellow employees was going through the wrenching process of separation and divorce, both of which were against his choice. He was trying desperately to persuade his wife to take him back. For weeks he talked incessantly of the effort he was making to change his wife's mind. We gradually grew indifferent to his crisis and became weary of hearing about his problem. After several weeks of failing to bring about a reconciliation, he grew very despondent and began to speak of suicide. Even this aroused no response from us. He was hurting and groping for comfort, but he received only indifference from us.

How unfortunate it is when we allow concern for our own affairs to shut out the needs and problems of those around us. How blessed we are to have an Elder Brother who "descended below all things" so that He could understand our sorrows and fears, and by understanding, care for and comfort us.

My friend finally made one last effort, pleading with his wife with all his heart for one more chance. She refused to even consider it and shut the door in his face. Broken-hearted and feeling that life was no longer worth living, he said good-bye to his two young children playing in the front yard, got into his car, and shot himself in the head with a shotgun in the driveway in front of his children.

Such a thing was incredible to me. How could anyone be so desperate? How could anything hurt that much? How could he do this in front of his children? The sorrow and hopelessness and worthlessness which he must have felt and which he had been trying to express to us at work was meaningless to me; it was beyond my experience and, therefore, beyond my comprehension.

After his suicide, I was assigned to take over his position at work. As I removed his belongings from the desk, I spent considerable time wondering in bewildered amazement that an intelligent, well-educated person could do such a thing. I never dreamed that I would one day be ready to follow his example, that I, too, would actually be tottering on the verge of suicide. I could not have believed that I would eventually find myself blankly going through the routines of each day, living from hour to hour, trying not to think, trying not to feel, just trying to survive—

But wondering why I should even bother.

II
From Seed To Harvest

THE SEEDS OF my excommunication were planted when I was a young boy. If the reader is to comprehend the events which led to my fall and excommunication, I must begin with a confession which may be offensive to some. I do this only to emphasize the power of moral sins to enslave us when we indulge the appetites of the flesh.

At the age of twelve I was taught a habit that would enslave me for over thirty years before it would be conquered. That habit was masturbation—a form of self-love. I was taught this sin by my father's best friend and employer. He told me that this act was necessary for my growth and development into manhood. He also warned me not to embarrass my parents by discussing it with them. (Years later it developed that this man was mentally ill and had abused several other boys. When he was finally discovered, he committed suicide.) I do not offer this explanation of the origin of my sin as an excuse. My conscience told me that something was wrong. Yet, in my youthful timidity and confusion, I never discussed my newfound knowledge with anyone. I abstained from the practice of it for a long time, but the day finally came when the urge to try it was too great, and natural curiosity overcame my apprehension.

The first time I decided to perform this act, I distinctly

heard a voice from the other side of the veil warn me not to do it but to go and discuss it with my father. Oh, how I wish I had heeded that warning! Instead, I chose to go ahead and experiment. That single seed of disobedience quickly blossomed into another, and another, until my harvest was a powerful habit. In a warped kind of perversion, this wicked form of self-stimulation seemed to provide a way to feel loved whenever I felt lonely or discouraged.

Naturally this secret and sinful practice caused feelings of guilt throughout my teenage years. Even though it was never mentioned at home or in Priesthood classes, my feelings of guilt grew and created within me a haunting sense of inferiority.

After graduation from high school, I joined the Air Force. There I began to grow and mature in the gospel. I fell in love with the scriptures. While others were running around town, I stayed in the barracks and studied the scriptures — often from six to eight hours a day. In the first six months, I read the standard works from cover to cover. The spiritual strength I gained from this concentration was a great help in trying to overcome my habit. The closer I grew to the Lord through the scriptures, the greater the guilt I felt when I did slip back into the sin.

Two years after joining the Service, I married. I thought that would surely bring an end to the problem, but because of my feelings of inferiority and guilt, I found it difficult to give or receive honest affection. Loneliness and discouragement continued to drive me back to the same form of self-gratification from time to time.

Then I discovered pornographic magazines. Viewing these added a new and highly addictive dimension to the temporary comfort and escape which my self-love had provided. I was now caught by a filthiness and carnality which had never been there before. My feelings of guilt from this indulgence were enormous, but the temporary "high" produced by the evil combination of self-love and pornography made it seem worth any price that must be paid. Like an alcoholic or drug addict, I was "hooked." I know that our Church leaders are totally correct when they warn that pornography is just as addictive and destructive as drugs and alcohol. Feeding upon its own awful lust, the viewing of pornography creates an ever-growing hunger for more and more filth. Like a run-away cancer, it is never satisfied but demands more and more until the victim can scarcely think of anything else. President Kimball has described the ever-increasing enslavement which pornography and self-stimulation commands in these words:

> Sin in sex practices tends to have a "snow-balling" effect. As the restraints fall away, Satan incites the carnal man to ever-deepening degeneracy in his search for excitement until in many instances he is lost to any former considerations of decency. (Spencer W. Kimball, *Miracle of Forgiveness,* First Ed., Salt Lake City, Utah: Bookcraft, Inc., 1969, p. 78.)

I tried very hard to overcome this growing addiction, but as the years passed, I became a living "Doctor Jekyll and Mr. Hyde" in my cycles of indulgence and repentance. There were two parts of me, both fighting for mastery. I felt desperate and was determined to conquer this problem. I was determined to live worthy of the Celestial Kingdom at all costs, but inside there was still a part of me that was equally determined to continue in the sin. Which part was really me? Which one would win?

For years I struggled, using every tool I could find. I read and studied the scriptures. I set goals. I filled my life with positive affirmations. I attended all my meetings. I served where allowed. I held consistent Family Home Evenings. I fasted and prayed. By exercising supreme will power, I could withhold myself from sin for several months at a time. But during these periods of abstinence the other part of me, the rotten part that loved the sin, would be growing stronger and more insistent. The pressure to give in was like water building up behind a faulty dam. The longer I abstained, the greater the pressure to give in.

In trying to describe this addiction, I realize that no one

will really understand it except, perhaps, former alcoholics or drug addicts. No matter how hard I tried to prevent it, sooner or later my resolve would weaken, the dam of my resistance would crack, and the accumulated pressure of months of abstinence would wash the dam of my will power away in a flood of indulgence. My evil surrender would last for a period of a few days or weeks until the filth of it would so thoroughly saturate my being that I could not stand myself. Then the magazines would be discarded, and a new cycle of repentance begun.

The grip of this awful desire was so great that when I passed an adult magazine stand, or saw someone reading such magazines, I would break into a cold sweat. My body would tremble, and my face would turn white. My heart would pound madly, and I would be totally consumed with desire. The only way to survive the onslaught of such attacks was to turn and literally run from the area. But even if I was successful in my escape, I would be haunted for days, wondering what I had missed.

One morning I arose early to do some yard work. As I took my first load of trimmings to the alley, I found two discarded pornographic magazines lying on the ground. I immediately began to shake and tremble, but somehow I managed to throw them into the bottom of the garbage can and bury them under the trimmings. Victory? No. I was so terribly haunted by what I had missed in those magazines that within a few days I gave way to the pressure of desire and fell into another cycle of indulgence.

My periods of repentance were sincere, fraught with great shame and remorse. I would fast frequently and pray constantly for deliverance. Trying to overcome my evil, I would submerge myself in the scriptures and church work almost to the point of fanaticism. I loved my opportunities for service in the Church and served faithfully in many positions. But always the righteous times were haunted by the threat of the pressure behind the dam of my will power, because, secretly, there was a part of me that still loved the sin. Eventually, no matter how hard I struggled to resist, the evil on the inside would win, and I would plunge into another cycle of sin. I now know that we never escape until we conquer.

These up-and-down cycles lasted through twenty years of marriage and eight children. During all this time, my wife stood by me, trying to understand and help. She was patient and forgiving, but it was not a problem that she could solve for me.

Eventually, the cycles grew farther apart, and my periods of righteousness lasted longer. I soon found myself serving in higher and higher responsibilities within the Church. But, as the years passed, the problem also grew more threatening. Each time I fell, my indulgence went deeper and lasted longer than before. I was even beginning to consider the idea of involvement with other women. Every time I fell, a part of me died. Each fall destroyed more of my self-image and made it all the harder to believe and hope that I could ever conquer myself. The shame and insecurity were devastating. It became harder and harder for me to decide which part of me was the Doctor Jekyll and which part was Mr. Hyde. I retreated into my own world of fantasy and filth, feeling so hollow and hypocritical that I wanted to avoid contact with everyone, especially my wife and children. My marriage got worse as I got worse. Everything got worse. My work suffered. My family suffered. I hated what I had become and what I was doing, yet I returned to it again and again.

I have told this part of my story to some who have responded by ridiculing my inability to overcome or control this enslavement. They have accused me of insincerity, stating that I only *believed* I was incapable of overcoming this sin and was, therefore, caught in a self-deceiving rationalization. In support of their accusations, they have quoted scriptures such as the following:

> There hath no temptation taken you but such as is
> common to man: but God is faithful, who will not

suffer [allow] you to be tempted above that [which] ye are able [to bear]; but will with the temptation also make a way to escape, that ye may be able to bear it. (1 Cor. 10:13.)

I do not condemn this reasoning, but I feel that those who think this way have grossly underestimated the power of sin. It is true that a neglected conscience will try to ease its pain through rationalization. It is also true that God protects us from trials and temptations which are more than we can bear, as testified in the scripture just quoted. Such protection is necessary to preserve our free agency, otherwise we could not be held accountable. But it is also true that when we deliberately and repeatedly choose to succumb to a temptation, we can lose or surrender our free agency. The weakness towards a sin or an addiction accumulates power over us as we give in to the habit again and again. This accumulated habit can eventually grow so strong that eventually we reach the point where we lack the will power, we lack the ability to reject our sin. We have forfeited our agency. The sin has become our master. This can happen with alcohol, with drugs, with pornography, with many things. President Kimball has referred to this condition of deliberate enslavement as "the point of no return."

It is true that the great principle of repentance is always available, but for the wicked and rebellious there are serious reservations to this statement. For instance, *sin is intensely habit-forming and sometimes moves men to the tragic point of no return . . .* As the transgressor moves deeper and deeper in his sin, and the error is entrenched more deeply and the will to change is weakened, it becomes increasingly nearer hopeless and *he skids down and down until either he does not want to climb back up or he has lost the power to do so.* (Spencer W. Kimball, *Miracle of Forgiveness,* First Ed., Salt Lake City, Utah: Bookcraft, Inc., 1969, p. 117; emphasis added.)

A man may rationalize and excuse himself till the groove is so deep he cannot get out without great difficulty. But temptations come to all people. The

difference between the reprobate and the worthy person
is generally that one yielded and the other resisted. *And
if the yielding person continues to give way he may
finally reach the point of "no return."* The Spirit will
"not always strive with man." (D&C 1:33) (Same as
above, p. 86; emphasis added.)

These are sobering words. They should cause us to
recognize the danger of tolerating any deliberate sin in our
lives. Who can afford to take the risk of becoming so
enslaved? Who can afford to be casual or careless about his
sins? Truly every decision, every choice, every sin does
count, and their power over us does accumulate. Consider,
therefore, the words of the Lord on this subject:

And behold I say unto you all that this was a snare
of the adversary, which he has laid to catch this people,
that he might bring you into subjection unto him, that
he might encircle you about with his chains, that he
might chain you down to everlasting destruction,
according to the power of his captivity. (Alma 12:6;
emphasis added.)

. . . and then is the time that they shall be chained
down to an everlasting destruction, according to the
power and captivity of Satan, *he having subjected them
according to his will.* (Alma 12:17; emphasis added.)

For behold, if ye have procrastinated the day of
your repentance even until death, behold, *ye have
become subjected to the spirit of the devil, and he doth
seal you his;* therefore, the Spirit of the Lord hath
withdrawn from you, and hath no place in you, *and
the devil hath all power over you;* and this is the final
state of the wicked. (Alma 34:35; emphasis added.)

But remember that he that persists in his own
carnal nature, and goes on in the ways of sin and
rebellion against God, remaineth in his fallen state *and
the devil hath all power over him.* (Mosiah 16:5;
emphasis added.)

Behold . . . thou art possessed with a lying spirit,
and ye have put off the Spirit of God that it may have
no place in you; but *the devil has power over you,* and
he doth carry you about, working devices that he may

destroy the children of God. (Alma 30:42; emphasis
added.)

. . . wherein *he became subject to the will of the
devil, because he yielded unto temptation.* (D&C 29:40;
emphasis added.)

I do not recite these scriptures to justify sinful habits or
to discourage the reader, but to emphasize our need for
divine help. Satan wants to persuade us that our sin won't
count or that we can "get away" with it this once, because he
knows that once soon becomes twice and quickly grows into
a habit. Because Satan and his evil spirits cannot enjoy the
pleasures that we experience through our flesh, they will do
all that they can to gain these fleshly experiences vicariously
through our bodies.

The Book of Mormon tells of a people who became so
enslaved by their sins that they forfeited their agency to the
point that they were in the total grasp of Satan's power.
Satan could, by that power which they had granted unto
him, cause them to perform sin when and where and how he
specified.

And thus Satan did lead away the hearts of the
people to do all manner of iniquity . . . the people
having been delivered up for the space of a long time
to be carried about by the temptations of the devil
whithersoever he desired to carry them, and to do
whatsoever iniquity he desired they should . . . (3 Ne.
6:16-17.)

Through my years of improper choices, I allowed Satan
to gain that same degree of power over me. I have
emphasized this throughout my story so the reader will know
that my eventual rescue and conversion was a miracle of
grace. Eventually I would learn that only God has the power
to change our nature so that we may then perfect our
behavior. Eventually I would open my heart to Him and
allow Him to work that miracle within me as I surrendered
my life to His will. But for now, I was blind to His powers to
help me overcome. I was buried in filth and degradation. I
was forty years old and fighting the same problem I had

begun at the age of twelve. Time was running out. When would this struggle ever end? I was without hope. What more could I do than I had already tried over all those dark, dark years? I was enslaved by an evil that was greater than my power or will to resist. I was about to encounter the next major change in my life, a change that would break every heart that had stood with me through all these trying years.

III
Deceived

THE JANUARY BEFORE my excommunication, I was deeply in debt and in desperate need of additional income. In addition to a full-time job at a Feed and Grain Store, which was physically exhausting work six days a week, I was attempting to sell Life Insurance and prepare Income Tax returns for over two hundred clients. My schedule began between 4:00 or 5:00 a.m. every day and never ended before midnight. By the end of the day, I was so physically and mentally exhausted that I would collapse on a bed which I had set up in my den. I slept there rather than competing with three little children who could never seem to make it through the night without joining Mommy. Also, I felt so evil because of my addiction to pornography that I didn't feel worthy to sleep beside her anymore.

By the end of each week, the paper work from the tax returns was piled so high that I decided to resign my church jobs and drop out of attendance, just until tax season was over, so that I could use Sundays as a catch-up day. This set a terrible example to our children. They were after me every Sunday. "Why aren't you coming with us, Dad? Please change your mind and come this time." My conscience was hurting, and finally, instead of repenting, I told my wife to "get those kids off my back or I am leaving home." The following is an excerpt from my wife's journal about trying to explain my threat to the children:

> Last night at Family Home Evening, while he was
> gone doing taxes, I tried to explain the problem to the
> children in a way that would be as compassionate and
> understanding as I could. I thought they were going to
> accept it reasonably well until our 12 year-old daughter
> realized what I was actually saying. Putting her face in
> her hands, she burst into sobbing over his decision.
> They were heart-broken.
>
> It was a hard thing to present in such a way that
> they would understand the mistake their dad was
> making, in deciding not to attend his Sunday meetings,
> without judging him or losing respect for him, but I
> felt they must know that it is a mistake. I never had to
> do anything more personally wrenching or difficult in
> my entire life!

I was about to learn the hard way that when one's life is
too busy for God, his life is just too busy. When a person has
no room for God or family, his life is too full of the wrong
things, and he is walking blindfolded in quicksand.

The inevitable result of this nineteen-hour schedule was
utter exhaustion, frustration, and disillusionment. It wasn't
long before I began to feel an enormous resentment of the
difficulty of supporting my family of eight children. Instead
of feeling like a father and a husband, I felt like a slave to
them. I became very resentful of the fact that no matter how
hard I tried, no matter how long I worked, I could never get
ahead of our bills and was lucky to even keep up. Even with
all this extra effort, I wasn't able to save anything towards
the $8,000.00 debt we had accumulated over the last few
years.

My wife and I had had problems in our marriage from
the beginning. We had married far too young. But, in
addition to our immaturity, there was the complication of
my periodic return to pornography and self-stimulation. I
often felt disappointment and resentment for what I thought
were her failures as my companion when, in reality, the
fault was mine. I can see now that all those invisible barriers
which she built around her tender emotions were necessary

to protect herself from the wounds inflicted by my periodic falls. After eight children and twenty years of ups and downs, we were both discouraged. I grew more and more indifferent and careless about our marriage relationship. Sadly, we were learning to live with a hollow, empty relationship.

Dropping out of Church was a fatal mistake. It quickly led to giving up on scriptures and prayer. Once those three steps were taken, I had opened the door to more of Satan's influences. As the tax season continued, I felt miserable and hopeless, and into this void came Satan with his vicious lies. He began by reminding me of all my moral failures. He reminded me of how earnestly I had tried to overcome pornography and self-abuse over all those twenty-eight years. He reminded me of how lonely I felt and of how unlikely it was that I would ever find happiness with "this wife." He reminded me of how resentful I was that she had never become my "dream girl" nor given me the happiness that I deserved. He whispered, then shouted, many things to my tired and attentive ears, and I believed everything he said.

The most vicious lie of all was that there are three kinds of people: celestial, terrestrial, and telestial and that I would never become a celestial person. Over and over he asked when I was going to face up to this reality and quit torturing myself? Why was I making my life so miserable by trying to be more than I really was? Didn't the last twenty-eight years prove that I would be much more comfortable and, therefore, much happier in one of the lower kingdoms? Doesn't the scripture say we are supposed to obtain joy? And wasn't it about time I started giving in a little and living for myself? After all, I could still serve and be of use in doing good in one of the lower kingdoms. Giving up on the Celestial Kingdom wasn't like I was admitting failure or something degrading. All it meant was that I was finally going to admit that most of me was pretty darn good except for this one minor moral problem, and so what? Who really cared about me, anyhow?

In other words, Satan deceived me into believing that if I would give up, I would still inherit all the joy I was capable of experiencing while eliminating the pain and frustration of trying to force perfection on myself. I suppose it sounds amazing that a person could actually believe such lies and distortions, but I had long since forfeited any claim upon the Holy Ghost. It was a long time after the court before I realized that I had actually been deceived. Until that time, I thought I had merely made some mistakes; I thought my problems were the result of poor judgement. It was very unnerving to discover that my thinking had not been clear, that I had actually been tricked.

Left on my own, without the Holy Ghost to guide me, my thinking was warped. In my desperation, I was ripe to believe anything that would make life seem easier. My self-image was shattered. In addition to economic failure, I was a failure in my marriage, in my family, and in my morals. I felt that I was a *total* failure. I believed everything Satan whispered in my ear. Thus, over many weeks I began to yield to this treacherous "way out" that Satan provided. He grew more and more bold until he was shouting at me every waking moment that giving up was the only way to real peace. I was agreeing with him without realizing my deception.

As I spent all of my emotional reserves on trying to survive economically, I retreated into my own miserable world, leaving my wife and children on the outside. The hollow emptiness which this action created finally led me to conclude that I should leave the family and strike out on my own. Surely there must be something better than all this, I thought. It wasn't that eternity and exaltation didn't matter to me anymore. I still had a testimony that the Church was true. I just didn't feel like I could live up to it anymore. I felt myself being pulled apart by the run-away-from-it-all emotions on one hand and the pull of loyalty and duty on the other. I felt incapable of coping with it anymore. I wasn't ready for divorce—that was too big a decision. I just felt that

I needed to get away for a few months by myself and think things out. The more I thought about it, the more I decided that I owed it to myself to escape this "slavery" and find a life of my own. What selfishness!

I hadn't figured out how to tell my wife, but she soon sensed the change in me and insisted on a heart-to-heart talk. She absolutely refused to accept the idea that moving out was a solution. She was totally convinced that if I would only promise to stay until May 15th, a month after tax season ended when I could slow down, everything would work out. Surely, she reasoned, if we worked together, we could somehow resurrect the love which had almost died from neglect. I disagreed, feeling that the separation was inevitable and that prolonging it would only increase her hurt when it finally came. But it seemed so important to her that I reluctantly agreed to wait. I was just too weary to protest.

Oh, how carefully Satan had wrapped his chains about me, and when I was sufficiently bound as to begin thanking him for it, he provided the opportunity to become involved with what seemed to be "the perfect girl." Thus my final fall came when I allowed myself to entertain the pleasant emotions which I felt in the presence of an attractive, divorced tax client. We felt drawn to each other, and in our mutual loneliness, we reached out, not to give, but to take from each other that which we felt we each needed and deserved. How cleverly Satan deceives us into believing that it is sudden love that we feel when all it really amounts to is lust and selfishness and a seemingly easy escape.

This woman and I had both failed in our marriages. Yet we thought that we "were made for each other" and that together we could build a wonderful new life. The infatuation which we felt for each other, the pleasure of escape from the reality of real-world responsibilities which we found with each other, seemed to be the most important thing in the world. To feel these new emotions seemed to be worth any price to make them mine forever.

Forever . . . there was the problem. I knew that this relationship could never be ours forever. No matter how wonderful life might be together in this world, I knew that it would have to end when death parted us. No, I had not forgotten the penalty for breaking temple covenants. Even at this point I knew that choosing to accept her love was a permanent and irrevocable turning away from everything — from my temple vows, my family, my testimony, the Church, and, of course, from the Celestial Kingdom. But I had closed my mind to all of that. Once I was convinced that I could never attain the Celestial Kingdom it seemed that I owed it to myself to reach out and grab this happiness for as long as I could. What selfishness! I no longer cared about anyone but myself. I didn't care about tomorrow anymore, only today. I had allowed myself to fall totally into the influence and illogic of the master deceiver. Step by step, compromise by compromise, I allowed him to wrap his chains about me. I am positive that he and his evil followers were rejoicing jubilantly as I accelerated my descent towards the final act.

Eventually I did what I had solemnly promised my God and my wife that I would never do. I desecrated the most sacred privilege that God has shared with mankind. Only then did I discover, when it was too late, what a shoddy and cheap imitation the devil offers. (One excommunicated person told me that following the act of adultery she heard loud laughter in the room. The room seemed to be filled with laughter, and, as the veil was taken from her eyes, she was allowed to see the dozens of evil spirits who were there, pointing in derision and laughing and rejoicing at the fall of another of God's beloved children.)

I saw no evil spirits. I heard no laughter. I just felt sick inside. The deed had been done. I had made my choice. The glitter of gold was gone. The ecstatic "live-happily-ever-after" dream seemed empty and far away. What had been done could not be undone. I had broken my vows. I was ashamed. I had deliberately followed Satan into sin, believing that I could turn and walk out on forty years of church and testimony and find peace and happiness. Satan had lied to me. I wasn't happy. I felt sick at heart. It wasn't worth it after all.

How could I have been so eager to trade eternity for now? How could I have been so blind as to think I could steal love from someone I didn't even know when I couldn't give it to the one that had loved me and stood with me through twenty years of loyal service and devotion? How could I have been such a fool? I had not been swept away with passion. I had deliberately and intentionally walked away from all that is precious and sacred and desecrated it with a stranger. And through it all, I thought only of myself. I thought only about what I would get out of it. To hell with everyone else, I had thought. And now I realized, too late, that it was going to be "to hell with me," and it wasn't even going to wait for the Day of Judgement. The day of judgement was right now. My conscience would not be silent.

I realized I could never continue the relationship. It had to end. I had to go back. I could not walk out on family and testimony and God after all. Somehow I had to make it back. I came to realize that the gospel was in me too deeply to up and walk away from it all. How thankful I am for the good parents that gave me those deep roots. How I wished I had honored them. Somehow, I had to find a way to build a successful life with my wife and children. My eight children . . . children that I did not deserve. I sat on the motel bed and took their pictures out of my wallet. I looked at them one by one for a long time. I looked at my wife's picture . . . and then, I wept.

IV
A Letter Of Love

MY WIFE WAS blessed with celestial parents. During the stress of my dropping out of church and threatening to leave, she made a trip to their home seeking the courage and help to save our marriage. Her parents could have easily and justifiably been angry and resentful towards me. But being the kind of people they are, their concern was as great for my peril as it was for their daughter's. They wrote a letter to me and sent it home with my wife. Because I love and respect my wife's parents, this letter had a profound effect upon me. More than anything else that happened, this wonderful letter made me hesitate in the path I was taking. It contains some great lessons:

Dear Steven,

We have been enjoying our daughter's visit and are thankful she came. I want to let you know again that we love you and respect you for many of the very fine things you do, and have done, and for the very fine person we know you to be. I want you to know of our love and keep it in mind during the next few minutes as you read this letter. Sometimes we need to hear more than just love, and it is in my heart to say some rather strong things to you, but in love and understanding, and with the hope that you will open your heart to it and accept it as trying to help you rather than to chastise you.

The course you are now taking can result in serious self-doubts. I mean the bit about not praying, not attending your church duties with wholehearted participation. I don't know why you are doing this. Perhaps you don't either. But ask yourself with your usual honesty if it could be that by withholding yourself, you are trying to reprimand God for what He is allowing to happen to you.

Our daughter says you say you still know the Church is true, but that you seem to have given up caring. When a child is thus disappointed he picks up his marbles and goes home in protest. When will you pick up again, if ever? Will it be after God changes some of the conditions of your life you now resent? And suppose those conditions do not improve. What is the next logical step to follow? Is it to take up sin? I know of children who get back at their parents by such behavior. By extension I see it possible to do the same with God, our Father. We could say to Him, "Very well, if you do not care about me, then I don't care about myself or You."

I recall that although I paid my tithing and lived the Gospel fairly well, I had nothing but problems on the farm I bought. After a large down payment and all I had put into it, grubbing out the mesquite trees, leveling it, drilling a well, I had nothing but problems. For example: After a hailstorm that knocked out half of my first crop, my second year brought a sharp freeze. My farm was the only one in the valley that was seriously damaged by the hailstorm, and it happened while I was in Salt Lake City to conference. The second year's cotton crop had been examined by several competent men as in excess of $30,000 worth of cotton. After the frost I picked less than $6,000 worth. Then, to make matters worse, the government decided to ration cotton the next year, but hadn't announced how drastic it was to be. Hence, no bank was willing to lend money. A year earlier I could have borrowed $10,000 with no difficulty. At this time I couldn't even borrow $2,500, which would have been more than enough to save my farm. Also, the company I had bought my cotton-picker from got upset with the conditions and repossessed it.

When I worked at the ice plant, I took over a defunct milk business, built it up to a respectable income, bought the ice-plant and three houses for $100,000. It had been earning $25,000 yearly in ice sales. I had hardly made the transaction before the state moved the truck weighing scales from the state line eighteen miles to the west to the east side of town. A truck could no longer ice up as before because they had to keep weight down till they could pass the scales. Many were the trucks that stopped needing 3,000 to 4,000 pounds of ice, but couldn't buy it because they had to cross the scales. As my business died, I lost the ice plant after paying $40,000 on it.

Because I wrote a letter published in the newspaper decrying dishonest practices in the town's service stations, certain of the disgruntled men wrote letters to the milk company I worked for which were bitterly biased. They got employees in the stores to put some of my milk out in the sun for a day, then back in the store to sell to the customers as sour. Everything that could be done to cause me to fail was done.

During all this time I was in the Bishopric. My boys and I practically kept the ward and its welfare and budget by cutting and bailing paper hay and doing 80% of the irrigating and hoeing on the church farm. I sent three of them on missions, overlapping their terms twice. It would have been easy to lose heart and give up and quit. I told the Lord I was thankful for my blessings. Only one house burned down. We still had our health, our testimony, and the children were turning out to be true Latter-day Saints. I had much for which to be thankful. Not only so, but during the fire I burned my feet so badly getting the little girls out that the doctors told me I would have to have skin grafted on my feet. The Bishop and my son gave me a blessing, and my feet healed without even a scar. I know I was blessed in my misfortune.

I leased the "180 Camp" which included a store, a service station, and 20 rental cabins. I had it only a month when they by-passed the highway around me for over a year while they built an underpass and cloverleaf to enter the freeway. You can imagine what that did to my business for a year as the rent went on just the same.

Now I've outlined some of the things that have happened to me. Not to make anyone sorry for poor little me, but to point out that the things in life which really count have always been in my favor. It began to look like I would never succeed at anything and would always have my nose at the grindstone. Until the last year or two I have never been out of debt. And we had eight children to raise with me being the only bread-winner. I know how hopeless it can look at times. However, my misfortunes could have been so much worse. My children never missed a meal nor were they poorly clothed nor suffered any serious misfortune. Through it all we were highly blessed.

Remember the section in the Doctrine and Covenants where the prophet felt he had borne too much, and he was told by the Lord that his misfortunes were but for a moment and, if faithful, what great rewards were promised. That promise is to all who will endure to the end. We are not promised a life of ease or trouble-free existence. Instead, this mortal life was designed to give us the troubles by which we can grow.

Now, as I look at your life I don't see anything so terrible or world-shaking. You have lived with the respect and love of your fellow-members. I doubt your family has often gone hungry. They all have brilliant minds and faithful hearts. You have great reason to rejoice in the blessings Heaven has sent you. If you can't be thankful for these great blessings, you may be asking for more serious troubles to chastise and humble you. The sin of ingratitude is great.

I have admired the way you have kept at the job of providing for your family, and you have had quite a measure of success, and, in so doing, have had a lot of the "experience" the Lord told Joseph Smith he was getting. Don't give up yet or get to feeling sorry for yourself.

When I gave you my daughter, I didn't think life would be easy for you. But I didn't think you would be a quitter. When she came to me some years ago to see if she should leave you because you were not getting along well together and had problems, I advised her to go back and work it out together, and your super children would be a prize beyond value you could earn together. I have not wavered in that belief—I see it ever stronger today.

Now, my son, lift yourself out of your morass of troubles and be thankful for what you have. Ask the Lord to forgive you for temporarily losing sight of your great blessings. Lose yourself in service to others, and you will find great happiness in this life and eternal joy in the world to come. If you do not do this, I fear you will lose your testimony and be delivered to the buffetings of Satan. And if you think your lot has been hard, it will become vastly much more so and with little hope for eternal reward. How bitter is servitude to the Devil!

Don't overwork yourself to the point of exhaustion. In so doing you lose your perspective. Take time for the Sabbath. The example to your family is too precious to lose. God will fulfill you his promise to open the windows of heaven and pour out blessings. These may not be largely financial, but you will be taken care of. You have a wife and family who will stick with you and without complaint. These are blessings beyond the reach of many. Look at your financial struggles as opportunities, for that is what they are. Some of my happiest years were spent with my nose continually at the grindstone. Learn to live each day for itself. In other words, there is joy you are now missing that could be yours with only a change of attitude. Attitude is so important in finding joy. Do not look forward to different conditions to bring you joy. You will lose it in the searching. It could be yours right now and in your present circumstances if you can so order your thinking to embrace it. These are not just empty platitudes. They can and will work. They have done so for me, and I can promise you in the name of Israel's God they can work for you. If they are not now doing so, it is the fault of your attitude.

This has been a long letter. Perhaps I have missed the point. But I have tried in love to help you and raise your perspectives. I sympathize with you in your troubles, but remind you they are what you shouted for joy with Job to receive. They are what you came here for. Make the most of them or your blessings can be taken away. We love you, and we gave you our daughter. She is a prize worth a pearl of any great price. Cleave unto her. Your marriage is no worse than many and better than most, and it can be just what you are willing to pay for it.

I could say this so much better to you if we were together. I am no great sage, or terribly wise, but there are some things I know truly, and one is that you have been and are being greatly blessed. Don't slack off in the effort to live the Gospel. You will find out in great bitterness that you punished only yourself and not God if you let up now. And to the end you may do so, we earnestly pray for you. And send our love.

As ever,
Dad

V
Compromises

NO ONE JUMPS into an excommunication situation in one giant leap. This awful tragedy comes into one's life as the natural result of a series of compromises and improper choices. Step by step we descend towards the emotions and the transgressions that cause us to abandon our covenants and duties. As this descent continues over weeks and months, our thinking becomes distorted, and we lose so much of our perspective. Gradually, carnal pleasures or stolen affections seem to be more important than covenants, honor, and loyalty.

As I have looked back upon the events which led to my fall, I have identified twenty-two specific decisions that led to my transgression. Twenty-two pivoting points of decision where improper choices turned me downward and away from the Savior, toward the greedy clutches of Satan. Each compromise made the next one easier, until finally there was not even a hesitation before the final transgression. Many of these choices overlapped, and yet each one was a separate ingredient in my descent. Almost every choice was based upon selfishness and seeking for an "easier way."

1. I allowed my marriage to deteriorate. I deliberately chose to stop trying to make it work and to allow our relationship to disintegrate.

2. I allowed debt to place an extra burden upon our

finances. This created extra and extreme job pressures.

3. I chose to ignore the laws of physical and mental health. I overworked my body and mind to the breaking point.

4. I resigned from my church assignments.

5. I stopped attending church.

6. I stopped reading the scriptures.

7. I stopped praying.

8. I became preoccupied with myself.

9. I lost all appreciation for my blessings.

10. I began to resent the Church and my family responsibilities.

11. I allowed myself to become totally isolated from my family.

12. I began to brood and focus all my thoughts on my problems instead of looking for solutions.

13. I began to blame my wife for my self-imposed misery instead of accepting it as my own responsibility.

14. Instead of saying that I had failed in life, I came to believe Satan's lie that I was a failure. There is a big difference.

15. I began looking for escapes instead of solutions.

16. I began to justify my sins.

17. I mentally, then emotionally, accepted Satan's degraded picture of me in place of the divine potential which God sees for each of us.

18. I consciously gave up trying to overcome my faults. I accepted Satan's lie that I had "gone too far" and that exaltation was just too hard for me.

19. I deliberately entertained thoughts of leaving my family as an escape from responsibility.

20. I allowed my feelings to override my testimony and conscience.

21. I allowed the present moment to become more important to me than eternity.

22. I allowed an attraction for another woman to occupy my thoughts and desires.

How important it is to stay close to the Lord, the scriptures, the Holy Spirit, and to remain active in the Church that we may guard against those very first erosions of resolve.

Our thoughts have been described as the blueprints of our future actions. Each of these twenty-two choices represent seeds which can blossom into apostacy.

> Examine yourselves, whether ye be in the faith; prove your own selves . . . (2 Cor. 13:5.)

> . . . pray always lest that wicked one have power in you, and remove you out of your place. (D&C 93:49.)

VI
The Break

MAKING THE DECISION to go back to my family was not easy. Saying good-bye to this girl was even harder. She was hurt, and she was furious. We had promised each other that we were going to build a wonderful new life together, and here I was telling her good-bye before it had scarcely begun. After making sure that I knew what a despicable creature I was, she stormed out of the motel. It hurt me to hurt her so abruptly, but there is no painless way of ending such relationships. As President Kimball has advised, the only successful way to repent of infidelity is with a total and abrupt divorce from all contacts and associations. While his advice may seem cruel and hard, I learned that it is not just the best way, it is the only way. We cannot repent as long as we insist upon compromise.

> . . . the devil knows where to tempt, where to put in his telling blows. He finds the vulnerable spot. Where one was weak before, he will be most easily tempted again.
>
> In abandoning sin one . . . should avoid the places and conditions and circumstances where the sin occurred, for these could most readily breed it again. He must abandon the people with whom the sin was committed. He may not hate the persons involved but he must avoid them and everything associated with the sin. He must dispose of all letters, trinkets, and

things which will remind him of the "old days" and
the "old times." He must forget addresses, telephone
numbers, people, places and situations from the
sinful past, and build a new life. *He must eliminate
anything which would stir the old memories.* (Spencer
W. Kimball, *The Miracle of Forgiveness,* Salt Lake
City, Utah: Bookcraft, Inc., 1969, p. 171-172; emphasis
added.)

As she stormed out of the motel, I thought to myself:
*Now I have messed up three lives: my own, my wife's, and
now this girl's.* Three lives, indeed! I had no idea how the
painful effects of this evil would penetrate the hearts of my
children, my parents, and brothers and sisters on both sides
of the family, as well as my friends in the Church. Perhaps
one reason immorality is such a serious sin is that it affects so
many innocent lives.

To say that I felt confused and miserable as I sat there
alone is completely inadequate. I had made the break, and
now I could begin to figure out how to go back to a wife I
didn't think I could love, and how to go back to a church I
didn't think I could live up to. My motives were weak, but at
least they were pointing me towards duty and repentance.

Still sitting there, I thought I had made my choice and
that I was on my way back. I thought my resolve was firm,
but I was soon to discover how weak I was. Duty alone will
seldom command obedience. There must be a foundation of
love and loyalty, or the call of duty will be drowned in the
clamor of escapes and seemingly easier ways. I discovered
this when the girl came back to the motel, crying that she was
sorry for all those names she had called me. She had decided
she was not going to let me go. "We just have to stay
together," she cried. "We could make each other so happy.
We need each other; we deserve each other," etc.

Those flattering words were tempting, but I was determined to resist, or so I thought. All the next day, as I went
about my business, I kept telling myself that I had made the
right choice and that it was my duty to stick by it. It was
going to be hard, but somehow I had to go back to my family

and my church and my testimony. Over and over I tried to reassure myself. But the emotional pull towards her was stronger than my resolve. By that very first evening I wanted to go back to the girl so badly that I just couldn't resist. I was being ripped apart between the call of duty and the call of worldly pleasure. I couldn't stand the torture any longer.

I was supposed to be doing income taxes, but I ignored my last appointment and parked by a canal bank where I could walk alone. I wanted desperately to pray for help, but I was too ashamed to pray. I had not prayed for so long, and now, after my sin, how could I dare to approach God for help?

I continued walking and fearing and sobbing until I finally could stand it no longer. I burst forth with an expression of sorrow for what I had done. I explained how I had messed up everybody's life and that I just didn't know how I could withstand the temptation of going back to that girl. I just had to have help resisting, or I would slip back to her in spite of my resolves.

The moment I finished my tormented plea for help—that very instant—the Lord's answer was there. Instantly His voice was in my mind, soothing me and reassuring me that I was not alone. His peace encompassed me and soothed my fears, witnessing to me that I was still loved. Loved? Yes! Loved no less than before I had committed this terrible act. The message was as clear and unmistakable as if He had appeared before my eyes in the flesh. There was absolutely no doubt that He had heard my prayer. Again I wept, overwhelmed by His response.

But God always puts a price on repentance. We must conform to His rules if we are to have His help. It must be done in His way, or we are left to ourselves. He is the Master. His way is best. His way may seem the hardest, but it is always the easiest in the long run.

And so, now came the challenge. Now came the test. "Steven, are your sobbings to me from a repentant heart or from the misery of vacillation?" He reminded me of the scripture:

> By this ye may know if a man repenteth of his
> sins—behold, he will confess them and forsake them.
> (D&C 58:43.)

*If you mean what you say, you will go home right now
and tell your wife everything,* He said.

I was horrified. "I can't do that," I cried in protest. "Not
now. Let me go home and work on making things right first.
Later, after my wife and I have made some progress in our
marriage, after I've given her something worthwhile to hang
onto, then I'll tell her."

You must go now, the command repeated. *It is the only
way.*

"But I can't do it now," I protested. "It would be so
cruel. It will crush her. Give me time—time to get strong,
time to reduce her hurt," I pleaded.

But over and over the answer was the same, only
stronger and stronger until I was practically pushed into my
car, and I headed for home—for home and for broken hearts
and, eventually, for repentance.

VII
Broken Hearts and Forgiveness

I HAVE SPENT considerable time relating my anguish. I have explained the mistakes that I made, the incorrect choices and compromises which led to my fall. I have explained my struggle to choose the right and how Heavenly Father was there with me instantly, ready to help once I was ready to repent.

Now I must tell the effect this had on my wife. The reader can easily imagine the agony that I caused her when I returned home with my confession. After all her years of loyalty and patience, after standing by me in spite of my pornographic cycles and indifference to her and the children, after all that sacrifice, I had finally betrayed her in the worst way possible. Yet, her great spirit was able to look beyond her pain towards choosing the right. There was never a moment's revenge or reprisal. Her utmost desire in working through this situation was to be in harmony with the Lord's will for the family. She felt that whatever that meant, whether it was a divorce, or still further forgiveness, her duty was to find His will and do it. How blessed I was to have such a noble wife. How blind I was to have ever been insensitive to her loyal support and love.

So that the reader may feel of my wife's spirit, I will now quote part of a letter which she sent to her parents informing them of the tragedy and how she felt about it. It is not easy for us to be this open and frank. We have done it in hope that others who are struggling through similar circumstances might receive hope and encouragement. Our witness to all is that when a person will surrender his ruined life to the control of the Lord, he will be wisely led to a successful healing.

When I exacted the promise from Steven that he wouldn't leave our family before May 15th, he gave it to me on condition that I would allow him to get away for a day or two if he felt he needed it. Being so confused, he felt he needed it now, so I consented. He got a motel room and stayed away Sunday, Monday and Tuesday nights. Wednesday he came back with the announcement that he'd made his decision and that he was ready to try again. He brought me a beautiful vase of flowers because I was sick and in quite a lot of pain. Then he left to go to his tax appointments for the day.

When he returned late that evening he paced around the bedroom; then finally, as he lay down beside me, he began to cry with great racking sobs, saying over and over, "I can't do it, I just can't do it." I didn't know what was happening, and I tried to comfort him. Finally he was able to quit crying. Then he told me. He said he had fallen deeply and desperately in love with another woman, a tax client, and that he had been unfaithful to me.

Mom and Dad, there is no human expression of emotion adequate enough to express the hurt feelings of horror and anger I had then. I cried, but not like you might think I would. I didn't scream or yell, I just hurt as he told me of his terrible struggle to decide whether to confess and come back or to stay with her. He asked me if I'd take him back. I asked him if he was willing to come back all the way—into the Church and family as well as to me. He said he was.

All my married life I've thought that if my husband was ever unfaithful to me, the marriage would end, and justly so. I knew I'd never be able to make love to him again, and I felt divorce would be the only right answer. But all I could think of then was that Heavenly Father still loves him and that we are commanded to forgive every man his trespasses. I was hurting so badly that all

I wanted to do was turn to God, who loves me, and do as I thought He wanted me to do, for I knew I could obtain surcease from pain and feel peace in only that way. Heavenly Father blessed me that my love for Steven didn't die. I knew that if he was truly repentant and willing to pay the price, my duty was to stick by him.

I asked Steven to give me his word of honor that he would never see or communicate with the other woman in any way ever again. He said he couldn't make that promise. He said he loved her so much he could not bear that thought so soon. I told him that our future hinged on that and on his willingness to pay the price of total repentance. Then I went downstairs to call the Bishop to ask him for an appointment the first thing next morning. He said he'd come by the house, and I told Steven he had until then to decide. We parted then—he went upstairs and I downstairs to spend a long, lonely, sleepless night.

By morning Steven had realized the wisdom of the commitment I was requesting of him and gave me his word never to see the other woman again. He made his confession to the Bishop. As soon as the Stake President gets back from Salt Lake City, I guess we'll hear what is to happen and when. The pain and embarrassment that is to come will be nothing—well, almost nothing—to what we've already suffered. I'm prepared for it mentally, and I am willing to suffer it if it will make us whole again. I'm only scared and sorrowful at having to tell the children. I trust that when that time comes, the Lord will show the way.

Now, Mom and Dad, I want to tell you one more thing about this, and I hope you won't be offended by the intimacy of it. After the Bishop left and our course was set, I realized my lot was cast with my husband's. He had said he'd give me all the time I needed before we made love again, but the time came sooner than I expected. He didn't insist, but I knew what he felt and that he wanted to make things right between us. I struggled with myself: "Should I give in so quickly? Shouldn't he be made to wait longer? It's not fair that he sins like that and then expects me to welcome him right back! He needs some kind of disciplinary action from me, doesn't he?" But that's not forgiveness, is it? The scriptures say, "Vengeance is mine." If that is true, then God will mete out the punishment more justly and fairly than I could, and I wouldn't have to worry about it at all. Forgiveness means no grudge, no recriminations, no withholding love. And so I came to a decision. In my mind I said, "Dear Lord, the burden is yours. I forgive him totally and completely, and all the rest remains with you."

Mom and Dad, it was almost physical — that transference from me to Christ of the hurt feelings and fear and even self-righteousness I'd been feeling. For the first time in my life I have come to truly appreciate and understand what His Atonement means to me!

In those minutes I understood Christ's love and the power of His Atonement as never before. It is difficult to express accurately — I hope you understand.

The future? I'm not naive enough to think it is going to be easy, for I know there will be some very trying times ahead. And I'm not saintly enough to keep the sordid aspects of it continually at bay in my mind. Christ didn't promise an easy time — just that His burden and His yoke are easier and lighter than any we might choose for ourselves.

I know you both love me and are hurting with me. But it is not the end of the world. We can go forward, and if you'd like to tell me your feelings, I would appreciate a letter.

Sincerely,

VIII
Round One

SEVERAL DAYS AFTER I returned home and confessed, an event occurred which left me trembling in absolute terror. The cause of my fear was a direct manifestation of Lucifer's power to destroy me now that I had become subject to his buffetings.

My wife and I had been extremely cautious in the way we treated each other. There had been no disagreements or conflicts until this particular morning. Suddenly we found ourselves arguing in a heated debate over something that was totally trivial and unimportant. We allowed the disagreement to grow until we were very angry with one another. I felt pressured by time because I was late for an appointment. I had to leave. There was no time to resolve the conflict.

As I left the house, I was greatly alarmed over the intensity of our feelings. Suddenly my confidence that things were going to be all right between us plunged into a nerve-shattering fear and uncertainty that we could ever affect a reconciliation. It was obvious that both of our feelings were more sensitive than either of us had supposed. The barriers which we faced in reuniting ourselves were greater than we had realized—perhaps even insurmountable. I got into my car trembling at the thoughts of struggling through the day on this shaky foundation. How little did I suspect that I was about to discover real terror.

I drove the half-block from our house to a cross street and, incredibly, came upon the girl I had sinned with. She was here, a half-block from my home? We saw each other simultaneously and stopped our cars right in the street. In astonishment, I got out and walked to her car to ask what in the world she was doing here.

In the days following our parting, she had called for me on the telephone over twenty times. To refuse to talk to her was extremely difficult. Hanging up on her felt cruel, but it was not as cruel as it would have been to stay in contact. I had promised a total break, and I meant to honor my promise.

Now, as I approached her car, she tried to pull me through her window to kiss me. She immediately began to plead for a chance to win me back. She insisted that she wanted me badly enough to actually come to my house!

I tried my best to ignore her pleading. I attempted to reason with her, but she began to cry, and I found my heart melting for her. At this point I had not yet seen our relationship as something as terribly wicked as it really was, and I was fresh from the disconcerting argument with my wife. I came within a hair's breadth of yielding to her pull, reversing my effort to confess and repent. I could hear voices echoing in my mind, urging me, *Go with her. Go with her. You deserve it. Go with her and be happy.*

Her pleading was almost more than I could bear. She was crying, but somehow, I found the strength to tell her angrily that it could never be. She must never ever contact me again. I walked back to my car and drove away. Now I was crying, too.

I was totally shaken. I was frightened by my susceptability to her invitation. I was shaken because of my reaction to my wife as well as to discover that my commitments were no stronger than a fractured eggshell. I was terribly confused and disoriented, but I was yet to meet the real terror.

About two hours later, lights began to flash and bells

rang in my mind. Suddenly I recognized the incredible timing with which that seemingly coincidental meeting had just taken place. Had I left my house one minute later, the woman would have been at my front door in confrontation with my wife! Had I left ten seconds sooner, I would never have seen her coming. The timing was, in itself, incredible, but for this to have occurred immediately following our first argument caused me to break into a cold sweat. I knew with positive certainty that this had all been engineered by Satan. I shrank in terror as I recognized his awesome power. His buffetings were not to be a series of mere temptations or trials. This was to be all-out war!

Talk about kicking a guy when he's down! I could see there would be no fair play in this contest. Satan had all the weapons, and, without the Holy Ghost or the Priesthood, I was unarmed.

How could he move upon this woman to travel clear across town — over half an hour's drive — to arrive at my intersection with such split second timing? Or, seeing her already on her way and recognizing her intent, how could he then take advantage of her coming by nudging my wife and me into a fight that would end at exactly the right instant? Or did he plan and inspire both events to occur in such a way as to almost surely break my resolve? Whichever way he had done it, I knew with a sickening feeling of fear that he was the one who had engineered it, and now I met the awesome terror of discovering the power and determination of my adversary. Imagine the feeling I had of realizing that I had months and perhaps years ahead of me to face such an enemy, without the Priesthood, without the Holy Ghost. I was absolutely terrified.

I share this experience for the sole purpose of convincing the reader that we are not discussing a minor confrontation. The excommunicant (and his family) must be aware that he is being plunged into mortal combat. His opponent is deadly serious and deadly accurate with his blows. Absolutely no one will ever escape this war until he cleanses his life, repents of his sins, and surrenders his life to the Lord who is waiting anxiously to bring him back to the fold.

IX
A Court For Me? No Way!

AFTER I RETURNED to my wife and confessed my adultery to the Bishop the next day, I was sincere in my intention to repent, so I never dreamed there would be need for a Church court. What for? I was firm in my resolve to avoid further contact with the other woman and equally determined to conquer my addiction to pornography, even though I had not confessed that part to the Bishop. I fully expected to be placed on probation until I had proven my sincerity, but I was absolutely stunned when the Bishop called to inform me that there would be court action. In past years, both as Bishop and ward clerk, I had participated in several courts that tried wayward Saints for their membership. Now I was to be tried? I was struck speechless.

At this point I had no realization of the gravity of what I had done. I had, of course, heard all my life that adultery was second only to murder, but what I had done seemed different. I just didn't see it as evil yet. To me, at that point, it had been a beautiful experience with a beautiful person. Of course, I knew it was against the rules, and I was sorry; but after all, I was back, wasn't I? I had chosen to remain in the Church and try to do my duty to my family, hadn't I? So why did we need a court? Why did we have to make it public and embarrass everyone? Ah, pride! I had much to learn before I would come to feel and accept "the full diabolical weight" of my sin, as President Kimball has described.

As the days passed, I fell victim to Satan's promptings and grew very rebellious. *What right do they have to drag you into court?* he taunted. *You came back voluntarily. You confessed voluntarily. You promised to repent voluntarily. You don't need a court to turn you around.* Then he suggested: *If they are going to excommunicate you anyhow, you might as well go back to the other woman and be happy.* The communication lines between Satan and me were very open in those days, but, of course, I didn't realize it at the time. Over and over, these thoughts ran through my mind. The more I thought about it, the more indignant I grew. *Well, I just won't even go to their silly court if that's the way they want to be,* I told myself. *I'll show them!* The more I thought about the embarrassment and humiliation a court action would cause, the more I rebelled. I wanted out. I wanted to run and hide. How sad it is when we allow our pride to make us more concerned about public opinion than about really repenting and making our life right with God . . . on His terms.

As I continued to struggle with these rebellious feelings, my Bishop gave me a copy of a talk on Church Courts and excommunication by Elder Robert L. Simpson as found in the July, 1972 *Ensign,* pages 48 and 49. This talk really did me a lot of good. It helped me to see my situation more clearly and to see the position of the Church which I had desecrated by my unworthy actions. It completely changed my attitude about the coming trial.

During the weeks waiting for my trial, I also read President Kimball's book, *The Miracle of Forgiveness,* again. I had read it once, several years before. At that time it had no significant impact on my life, but now I saw it from the perspective of one in desperate need of hope, and it was like pure water to my aching thirst. Then I read it again, this time filling a notebook with quotations of those parts which seemed most applicable to my situation. This study convinced me that I had done something far worse than I had ever dreamed. It helped me to see my sins from God's perspective. I began to realize how horribly I had offended Him by violating my covenants. I began to see how crucial it was to subject myself willingly to the justice of His prescribed (and required) legal court procedures. I realized the court was not intended as discipline or punishment, but rather it was to teach me of the supreme importance of God's laws which I had so carelessly cast aside. I came to realize that the court was there to help me start on the long road back to Him. I now realized that I had to walk that path using God's way and according to His divine wisdom instead of trying to make it back by my own short-cut methods.

As my attitude about the court began to change, I thought a lot about the secrecy of my past sins. I thought about how I had struggled with them over and over through the years, without really confessing them to a Church authority. I had never lied about my worthiness. I just made sure that I had abstained from my habits long enough to feel clean when I went in for temple recommend interviews and such. And then I remembered the scripture that said God judges the sincerity of our repentance by two standards: first, by the fact that we confess our sins, and secondly, that we forsake them. (See D&C 58:43.) Could it be possible that allowing my pride to prevent my confession through all those years had something to do with the perpetuation of my weaknesses for so long? Had I unwittingly prolonged the struggle by trying to short-cut the confession part of repentance?

Suddenly I could see that it was a form of pride which had convinced me that I didn't need the confession part. I had been too proud to reveal my dilemma. Because I had refused to repent the way God required that one should, He had left me to myself to struggle until I finally learned that He really does know best. One thing was for sure: it was utter foolishness to keep hiding all that filth inside of me, allowing it to rot and fester and poison me. As I studied President Kimball's book, I came to see why confession is an essential part of the Lord's purification process.

I needed to confess and, finally, I knew it. I would do it. I would confess everything. Even though the trial was scheduled on the basis of my recent adultery, there was a lot more sin inside me that no one knew anything about. I would come clean and tell all. If confessing it all could start the process of emptying the filth from my mind and body, thus making room for the Holy Spirit, I would gladly do it. I wished I had done it long ago.

I began to look forward to the court. I could hardly wait. I knew when the brethren in my trial heard my full story, I would be excommunicated for sure, but that was what I deserved and needed. For once I was going to be totally open and honest about everything.

I am so grateful that it took several weeks for my court to be scheduled, because this waiting period gave me time to learn the truth about the court's purpose. During this time, I was able to overcome all those nasty, bitter feelings of resentment and petty embarrassments that Satan had whispered to me. For once I was going to be totally square with the Church. Somehow I sensed that this would not be the end for me, but a new beginning, and I was anxious.

X
The Court

ON THE APPOINTED evening, my wife, my Bishop, and I went to the Stake Center for the trial by Church Court. There convened were twelve High Councilors, the Stake Presidency, and one Stake Clerk; sixteen brethren with whom I had served in various positions. The High Councilors were not informed as to who was to be tried until the court actually convened. As my wife and I entered the room where they awaited us, I could see the shock and pain in their faces as they discovered that it was me to be tried. After that first glance, they very politely avoided looking at me, a consideration which I certainly appreciated.

I could hardly believe the spiritual power I felt in that room; it was overwhelming. Sixteen righteous, dedicated men were gathered there to perform a duty required of them by the Lord. It was obvious during the entire procedure that this was an extremely painful experience for them, something they were required by their calling to do, but which they disliked and would have preferred to avoid.

In addition to the overwhelming power of their accumulated priesthood, I felt the added power of the love that emanated from them. How many Sunday School and Priesthood lessons had I heard through the years which explained that Church Courts are courts of love? It is true. I knew that I was in this court to be judged, yet there was absolutely no feeling of judgement, scorn, or disdain present there. I felt completely comfortable and safe in their hands.

The proceedings were simple. After we all knelt around the table for a most beautiful and touching prayer, pleading for the Lord's spirit to guide the affairs of the court, the Stake President explained the charges and asked me if they were true. I acknowledged that they were. He then gave opportunity for my Bishop to comment and allowed my wife to express her feelings. Then I was allowed to speak. I was told that I could say whatever I wanted in regard to this transgression and any others that I felt were pertinent to the decision of the court.

As I began my confession, I felt a very heavy burden lifting from me. With each confessed sin, the weight of my guilt seemed to lighten. Feeling nothing but love and sorrow from the members of the Court made it easy for me to be open and honest. I confessed my adultery as well as the struggles I had endured since I was twelve years old. I confessed my cycles of addiction to pornography and subsequent efforts to repent and free myself of that awful taskmaster. I confessed the "adult movies," the massage parlor, everything. The only response was a clear expression of compassion and sorrow for what I had suffered. I want to emphasize that there was not the slightest trace of criticism or condemnation. Truly, it was a court of love.

After I had made a full confession, I was asked if there was anything else that I should mention. What a truly great relief it was to be able to say, "No, that was everything." I felt as though an enormous weight had been lifted from my shoulders. After my confession came a period of open questions. Again I was shown the utmost respect and courtesy. Then the Bishop, my wife, and I were dismissed while the brethren deliberated on the verdict.

I was amazed that they took well over a half hour to discuss the case and weigh the alternatives. Obviously, they did not take their duty lightly. After what seemed an eternity of waiting, we were invited back, and the verdict of excommunication was explained to me in detail. After a closing prayer, the brethren were immediate in their efforts to express their love and support. In the coming years every time I saw one of these brethren, they were always eager to shake hands with a special eye-to-eye expression of warm love and support.

I came away from the Court with a new appreciation of the Lord's concern for us. His laws are clear and precise. The rewards for obedience are clearly enumerated, as are the penalties for transgression. In His love and mercy towards us, He has clearly outlined the necessary procedures so that a person may have the satisfaction of going before His legal representatives and receiving an official judgement. To know exactly where I stood and to know exactly what would be required for me to work my way back was a wonderful relief. How blessed we are that these definitions and guide-lines are clearly established. How awful it would be to have them left to the opinion and whim of man. There was absolutely no question about the justice of my verdict. I knew that it had been a matter of prayer and revelation; I knew it was the official word of the Lord to me, and I felt totally right about it. The letter below was mailed to me the next day to confirm the verdict and summarize the restrictions which were now placed upon me.

> Dear Brother Cramer,
>
> This is to serve as formal notice of the results of the High Council court held in your behalf. Since you were present, you already know that it was the decision of the court that you be excommunicated from the Church of Jesus Christ of Latter-day Saints.
>
> As you know, excommunication means complete severance from the Church. You should remove your temple garments. You may attend Sacrament meetings, auxiliary meetings and Stake and General Conference sessions, but you will not be allowed to attend Priest-hood meetings[1] nor will you be allowed to speak in any

---

[1] Excommunicants are now allowed to attend Priesthood meetings, but of course, still are not allowed to participate.

of the meetings.

I hope you realize that those of us who were there stand ready to assist you at any time to help you in your progress toward rebaptism into the Church. We express our best wishes for your future happiness.

Sincerely,

The first letter I had received to notify me of the pending court and trial had been met with tears of remorse, confusion, and bitterness. This letter, however, found me at peace because the matter had been settled. I was at peace because I was full of hope that I could now make a clean break from my past and grow towards a new life of purity.

I know that there are many in the Church who avoid confession to their Priesthood leaders (as I did) out of the fear of Church courts. This is most unfortunate, for it leaves the secret sin hidden within the individual where it rots and festers and deprives him of fellowship with the Holy Spirit. Eventually, if left unresolved, this attempted deception will result in permanent condemnation. The Savior warned us of the judgement which would befall those in His sacred Church who offend Him and pollute the Church by trying to short-cut His established procedure for repentance when He said:

> The Son of man shall send forth his angels, and they shall gather out of his kingdom all things that offend, and them which do iniquity;
>
> And shall cast them into a furnace of fire: there shall be wailing and gnashing of teeth. (Matt. 13:41-42.)
>
> But wo unto them that are deceivers and hypocrites, for, thus saith the Lord, I will bring them to judgment.
>
> But *the hypocrites shall be detected* and shall be cut off, either in life or in death, even as I will . . .
>
> Wherefore, let every man beware lest he do that which is not in truth and righteousness before me. (D&C 50:6, 8-9; emphasis added.)

All who are hiding serious sin cannot have confidence before God. Let us remember that Jesus Christ is perfect;

therefore, everything that He does, and everything that He reveals and commands is also perfect. He has established a judicial system as part of His perfect Church organization. We can have confidence, therefore, that in His infinite and perfect wisdom and love, the judicial system in this Church is the best, most effective procedure which He could possibly give us. If there were a better way of helping people who are guilty of serious transgression, He certainly would have revealed it. This one fact alone should give courage and confidence to all who become involved with Church courts, whether as administrators or as one on trial.

XI
Telling The Children

AFTER THE TWO-HOUR court proceedings, we returned home to our family. None of the children, except our oldest son, knew anything about my transgressions. None of them knew where we had been that night or why—we had only told them that we were going to "a meeting." My wife and I took our eighteen-year-old son and the two oldest girls, ages seventeen and fifteen, into the privacy of a room away from the rest of the family where I explained what I had done and that I had been excommunicated. They didn't know what that would mean, so I explained its ramifications and that it would take years to make things right and get back into the Church. I pled with them to remain strong and never let this happen to them. Both girls wept with us as they struggled to comprehend the terrible significance of the unbelievable words they were hearing. All three of them put their arms around me and promised their love and forgiveness.

Then we took each of the middle children, ages seven, ten, and twelve, one by one and explained the situation, again asking each of them for their forgiveness and pledging my intention to repent and become a real part of the family. One daughter, the twelve-year-old, seemed to take it the hardest. (She was the one who had cried so hard when I had dropped out of church attendance.) She started crying and, thinking I had been excommunicated for not attending church, said, "I thought you had to do adultery or something serious like that." After explaining that that was exactly what I had done, she sobbed even harder. She just couldn't believe that her dad could have done such a thing. Later, while writing this book, I asked her if she had worried about what her friends might say or do. She said, "No way! All I was worried about was keeping you and Mom together so there would be no divorce."

Our son, who was ten years old at the time, said he thought that his sisters had done something very wrong and were in a lot of trouble because, as we'd talk to each one, they would come out of the room crying and looking so serious.

All of the children were fantastic. Not one of them condemned me or withdrew their love from me. They readily forgave me and pledged their support. They prayed for me; they believed in me; they tried to encourage me; and somehow, they managed to keep wanting me.

I asked each of the older children to tell me what advice I should put in this book to the children and families of others who were just learning about excommunication. They each took the question seriously and gave it much thought before responding. The consensus of their response is as follows:

1. Never give up hope.
2. Show your love all the time.
3. Let them (the excommunicant) know you are on their side.
4. Try not to judge.
5. Always stick by them and don't give up, or it will be a lot harder for him.
6. Be understanding. So a mistake was made. We all make mistakes. Show the same love and support as before.
7. Always pray for them.

My wife and I were very concerned for our children. We were fearful that their friends and classmates might avoid them or withdraw their friendship because of my excommunication. We did their friends an injustice by so thinking. They were great! Never once did anyone hurt our children or offend them because of my situation. In fact, just the opposite was true. Many, many times their peers expressed their love and support and encouragement.

XII
Adjusting and Coping

EXCOMMUNICATION IS NOT something for which any of us are prepared. Many difficult adjustments must be faced by the individual and his family when one is cut off from the Church. There are no easy answers or instant solutions. Healing takes time. If one is to be successful in repenting and making his way back into the Church, he must be willing to pay the total price no matter what it costs in personal change and no matter how long it takes to make those improvements in character, spirit, and behavior.

An excommunication is one of the most difficult challenges a family can experience. It is probably more confusing and difficult to endure than a divorce or death. Similar to divorce, sealing bonds are broken, relationships are strained, and barriers of separation are placed between the one expelled and those who remain inside the Church. Like the loss of a loved one in death, the excommunicant has literally died spiritually, yet he is still alive and present physically, and somehow the relationships must be rebuilt.

The problem is that the old ways of relating won't work anymore. There are new wounds on both sides—deep wounds. Feelings are tender. Both partners are filled with doubts about the future, doubts about loyalties, doubts about how much they can depend on each other, doubts about the sincerity of repentance, doubts about the honesty of forgiveness for the wrong which has come between them, doubts about their ability to understand and cope with the stress which has come into their relationship.

The members of the family will often wonder why they, the innocent ones, have to suffer so much when it was "he" or "she" that was cut off. They must learn that it was not just "he" or "she" but a part of "them" that was expelled. The family is in this together. When a branch is cut off from a tree, both the tree and the branch are injured. If the wounds are ever to be healed, it will depend greatly on how the family responds to the unjust suffering this person will inflict upon them. The Savior said that "inasmuch as ye have done it [or failed to do it] unto one of the least of these my brethren ye have done it [or failed to do it] unto me." (See Matt. 25:31-46.) The excommunicated person has suddenly become "one of the least of these." He will be judged and held responsible for what he has done, but the family members will also be judged by the way each member treats this person, by the way each relates and reacts to him. Here, in this painful life-and-death crisis, the family's Christianity will be tested to the depths. The family will be tempted to punish the excommunicant for what he has done. Satan will constantly try to destroy family unity by prompting the family to "get even" and to "make him pay" for what he has done. Satan will tempt family members to respond to the excommunicant in kind. That is to say, when the person is angry, resentful, bitter, unthoughtful, impatient, overly demanding, etc., they will be tempted to hurt him in similar fashion.

Guilt and punishment are difficult to deal with, especially when wounds are deep, but if the members of the family cling to their wounds, if they constantly remind themselves of the injustice of the situation, they will never be able to forgive. It is God's place to judge when the price has been paid. He has told us that those who refuse to forgive will bear the greater sin. (See D&C 64:8-10.) It is improper to condemn the excommunicant for his inability to repent instantly because others can never understand what he is going through unless they experience it for themselves. If those who are still part of the Church have trouble accepting and coping with the situation, try to imagine how painful and confusing it must be for the one who was cut off!

The excommunicated person desperately needs the family support if he is to be saved from what he has done and from what he has become. Of course, redemption is still possible even if relationships with the family are severed, but the path to recovery will be all the longer and harder to pass for both the individual and the family. The Lord needs the family to become the funnel through which He can channel His love for this person. The family needs to use its time and emotions to reaffirm constantly, daily:

1. We still love you.

2. We do not understand what you are going through, but it must be awful for you, and we want to help.

3. We need you, and we want you back as a part of us.

4. No matter how long this takes, you can count on us to see it through with you.

So much depends upon the family's relationship with the excommunicant. I urge you to make the Lord your partner in helping him. I know that the Lord is anxious to respond to such a request.

While the excommunicated person is allowed to attend most church meetings, there are many restrictions placed upon his participation. For example, an excommunicant is not allowed to speak or pray in church meetings. He cannot participate in classroom discussions. He is not allowed to partake of the sacrament. He cannot even raise his hand to sustain people in their new callings or to welcome new members to the ward. Each restriction requires the excommunicant to make new adjustments, adjustments which are often painful and discouraging, but which are part of the price to be paid for one's disobedience. What a terrible feeling it is to sit in classes week after week for months and years, yearning to participate, but forbidden to speak, pray, or even bear testimony. This is something I never got used to. How earnestly I wanted to belong, to be part of what was happening.

My first exposure to this feeling of isolation came even before my trial when our family attended an Easter Pageant. There, for two hours, while uncontrollable tears rolled down my cheeks, the Spirit bore witness to me that, because of my transgression, I had forfeited the most important thing in life: my relationship with the Lord and His Church. I came away from the pageant very depressed, sensing a loss I could not yet measure.

I was determined to manifest the sincerity of my repentance by faithfully attending 100 percent of all the meetings open to me. I expected to feel embarrassed, but I was totally unprepared for the devastating feelings which overwhelmed me as I entered the chapel that first Sunday after my excommunication was announced in Ward Priesthood Meeting. It was awful. As I walked in with my family, I felt totally naked and dirty—I felt filthy. It seemed as if every person in the congregation was staring at me and could tell how unworthy I felt. Of course, that was not true. I doubt if anyone stared, and they certainly could not know how I felt. Nevertheless, I wanted to turn and run. This was too hard. I wanted to escape, to just disappear, yet I knew that I had to stay and face it. I knew that if I left, it would be even harder to return later. So I stayed. Of course, such feelings of self-consciousness are only natural. I found that they diminished as I proved faithful in attendance and repentance.

I once had the privilege of participating in a panel discussion with a Regional Representative and about a dozen other excommunicants. One of the topics discussed was how we were treated by the members of our wards. It was made manifest by the discussion that most of us had been hurt by things which had been said or done at church. One brother, for example, told how often the members of his ward had looked upon him with scorn and disgust and then actually gotten up out of their seats to move to another location so they would not have to sit by him. What a tragedy that is! What a terrible indictment! I know that those who judge in this manner will one day face an angry Savior who has promised (warned) to return our unauthorized judgements upon us in kind.

I did not experience this rejection. Many people in my ward and stake went out of their way to shake my hand and to express their love. I think the only time the members of my ward really felt awkward around me was when I felt awkward about myself. I really believe that if the excommunicant builds a barrier to isolate himself from contact with other ward members, then they will sense it and hold their distance. On the other hand, if he is willing to be fellowshipped, the majority of the people will respond warmly.

How grateful I was to receive the following note from one of my ward members. What an encouragement this little note gave me. It helped to sustain me through difficult times, and it made me want to try harder to be what I needed to become.

> Dear Brother Cramer,
>
> I hope I don't embarrass you by what I say. I couldn't help notice your eyes water as the children were confirmed today. I want to tell you how your continued activity in the Church with your wonderful family strengthens my testimony. It makes me realize how precious membership in our Church is, and how it is really worth working for.
>
> I can hardly imagine what a struggle it would be to stick with it without the constant companionship of the Holy Ghost. I admire you so much for your effort. It must be a blessing to have your family around you.
>
> This Church is true and is worth working for. Your presence here today and each week is as much a sermon to me as any you could have spoken.
>
> L.R.

It was concluded by our panel discussion that most of the injuries and insults we had received as excommunicants were unintentional. We were asked how we dealt with such feelings. I love the brother who responded by quoting the following scripture:

> For if ye forgive men their trespasses, your heaven-
> ly Father will also forgive you:
> But if ye forgive not men their trespasses, neither
> will your Father forgive your trespasses. (Matt. 6:14-
> 15.)

He spoke for all of us when he said, "I need my Heavenly Father's forgiveness, and I will not allow another person's insult to become a barrier to that forgiveness. If I am to be forgiven, I must forgive everyone, no matter what happens."

Through working my way back into the Church I learned that the most important opinion is not that of the ward members, nor is it the opinion of one's family — important as they are. The only opinion that really matters is what the Lord thinks and feels about us. Nothing is more important to rebaptism and spiritual health than discovering the reality of His stubborn love which extends even to the excommunicant. The Savior wanted us to remember that "the Son of Man is come to seek and to save that which was lost." (Luke 19:10.) There is never a trace of condemnation in His perfect and unwavering love. Even though the excommunicant has lost the Holy Ghost, the Church, and the Priesthood, even if he has lost his family, the Lord is always there waiting and wanting to effect the miracle of His Divine healing. A person cannot be excommunicated from God.

That I was truly "on the outside" of God's Kingdom was really brought home to me when one of my tax clients opened a religious discussion with me.

"What church do you belong to?" he asked.

"I'm a Mormon," I said from habit but found the words choking in my throat. *Oh, no, you're not!* I heard shouting in my mind. *You forfeited the right to belong to My Church!*

As our discussion progressed there were many sincere questions asked. Here was a real opportunity to teach the gospel to someone who seemed to be open to the truth. I have served on three stake missions and spent many years teaching "Investigator" and "Gospel Essentials" classes. I know how to talk to non-members from their own bibles, but everytime I tried to expound a doctrine in answer to his questions, I found myself unable to speak. The words seemed to stick in my throat; I could hardly express myself. Louder and louder the accusation forced itself upon my mind: *You are not worthy to represent My Church! You, who have desecrated My Church, you have no right to speak on My behalf.*

I finally had to change the subject. I simply could not respond to his questions. It was as if my tongue had been struck dumb. This disconcerting experience taught me more than anything else that I was truly no longer a Mormon.

Another adjustment to this feeling of expulsion was the startling discovery that all my family sealing lines were broken. Naturally, our temple marriage was dissolved. This also meant that my children were no longer sealed to me. Unless that bond could be restored before death, my eternal family unit would stand in jeopardy, and I could be left outside the family circle forever.

The ties to my immediate family were not the only ones broken. The sealing to my parents, grandparents, brothers and sisters were also severed. Not only was I expelled from the Church, but I literally stood disconnected from all family ties. Everything was undone. Until one is rebaptized and temple blessings are restored, the excommunicated person literally stands alone. He doesn't belong to anyone. It is a terrible feeling to be so utterly alone.

One of the great losses resulting from the excommunication of the husband and father is the loss of the Priesthood from the home and family. This was a very difficult adjustment for me to make. Losing the Priesthood not only changed the spirit in our home, but it also caused a painful experience for me each time the Priesthood was needed for administration of the sick. (With eight children, this happened frequently.) When little children were ill and tear-fully told Mommy or Daddy, "I need a blessing," it was not only frustrating to have to call others to come to our home to perform the ordinance for me, but it also put serious confusion in the little children's minds. "Why can't Daddy do it?" I was always grateful for the brethren who came so willingly, but it was hard to stand aside while they pronounced the blessing which should have come through me as the Father.

Loss of the Priesthood, however, does not mean that we cannot pray and exercise faith over the needs of our loved ones. Prayer for a sick loved one is perhaps even more fervent when it cannot be supported with one's own anointing. Prayer alone should never substitute for official anointing by the Priesthood when it is available, but the excommunicated person can still gather his family and lead them in prayer to support and honor the administration of the Priesthood brethren who were called to perform the administration.

As an excommunicated person I was not allowed to pay tithing. What a frightening restriction this was. I never realized how strong the feelings of peace and security were that I had received from obedience to this commandment until I was denied the blessing. I dared not use that sacred tenth for personal needs. I had paid tithing all my life, and I could not stop now. I opened a special savings account and faithfully deposited my tenth there until I was rebaptized, at which time I closed the account and transferred the funds to the ward tithing account. What a wonderful feeling it was to bring that sacred savings of thousands of dollars and present it to the Bishop. It would have been far more difficult for me to feel right about coming back into the Church if I had taken advantage of the situation and used that extra ten percent for my own affairs. This action is not required of an excommunicant; it is strictly voluntary, but I felt that the law of tithing applies to all of God's children, not just to members of His true Church.

Another difficult adjustment for me was the Sacrament Service. I could always sense the curiosity of the deacons when I passed the sacrament tray to my family without partaking of it myself. My little children noticed it also. What does one say to a five-year-old when she asks, "Mommy, why doesn't Daddy ever take the Sacrament?" Excommunication is hard enough for grown-ups to understand. How can it be explained to a child?

Later, as I came to understand the atonement in a personal way, and as my repentance progressed, the Sacrament time became very significant in my life. Even though I could not partake of the bread or water, I could still pray and renew my personal covenants with the Lord. Once I stopped worrying about what others were thinking about me, I found the Sacrament to be a time when I could review my week, review my repentance and commitments, a time when I could reaffirm promises to my Heavenly Father, a time when I could pour out my heart in gratitude for His mercy, and a time when I could plead for strength, courage, and persistence to live more worthy before Him during the coming week. For the first time in my life, the Sacrament became a time to really sense the reality of the Savior's personal love for me and to feel the effect of His Atonement on my life. I often wept, and as I did so, each tear helped to cleanse my soul of all that was rotten inside.

I learned the hard way that each of the experiences I have described are part of the lessons which excommunication is designed to teach. I learned that we must accept such experiences as the Lord's way of teaching us, and also, that we must constantly be on guard to prevent these stressful situations from causing feelings of bitterness and resentment. Experiences such as those I have shared can drive a terrible wedge between the excommunicant and the Lord, or they can become positive motivations to live in such righteous obedience that he can find his way back into the Church.

We are in serious error if we think that we can make the

excommunication a comfortable experience. An excommunicated person is going to endure suffering; that is part of the repentance and healing process. It is a form of pride to believe that one can ignore God, that he can toss aside all that God is and all that He stands for and has offered us; it is pride to believe that one can do this in order to make his own way to happiness outside the boundaries of God's plan. Before the excommunicant can be healed, this arrogant pride and foolish ignorance must be broken and crushed by the things which he suffers so that he can see, even as a little child, that Heavenly Father really does know best after all. (See D&C 19:15-17.)

Following the excommunication, the person will feel totally confused and worthless. He will probably continue to suffer this darkness, pain, guilt, shame, hopelessness, and confusion until he comes to hate himself, until he comes to hate what he has become, and until he hurts badly enough to recognize his desperate need for a Savior. Alma's thoughts and desires would never have turned to Christ if he had not experienced such an unbearable horror in consequence of his sins. (See Alma 36:12-21.)

The family members, too, will experience many self-doubts and wonder just how much responsibility each of them shares in this person's failure. There is little profit and much harm in replaying the past over and over. We cannot change what is past, but we can start now to build a better future.

Those who try to help the excommunicated person to make his way back are often guilty of trying to "patch things up" with spiritual Band-aids when the real need is for major surgery. We seem to want to hurry and clean him up with a shining new paint job when what is needed is a dye that will soak clear through. It takes time to make a new creature of a person. He must be "born again" into a spiritual life of devotion to God and His laws. This birth process will be painful for both him and his family. Preaching or nagging while he is struggling to find his way is inappropriate. Allow the Lord time to work out the problems.

We cannot expect the excommunicated person to understand himself as he struggles through these changes. We cannot expect him to tell us what we need to do to help him — because he doesn't know. His vision is clouded, his judgement is distorted. This is a new and frightening experience for him, and he is groping in an unknown darkness.

At first the excommunicated person may be expecting the Church to rescue him from himself. When it does not do this (or even try to), he will likely feel even more abandoned and may easily become bitter and resentful. This response is most unfortunate and will only add to the pain and suffering to be endured before repentance and forgiveness can be found. I know excommunicants who have expected the Church to somehow nurse their wounds and restore them to spiritual health. This the Church cannot do. It is the individual's responsibility to repent and change his life. The Church provides the truth and the path to the Celestial Kingdom, but none of us will reach that wonderful goal if we refuse to move until someone holds our hand. The Church, itself, cannot save us. Only obedience and living of a Christlike life will purify us sufficiently to allow the Savior to apply His Atonement in our behalf. As he struggles to find his way back to the Father, the excommunicant must learn to focus his repentance on building a spiritual relationship with the Lord and not worrying about what others are doing or not doing for him.

The excommunicant should resolve to attend every church meeting possible. He should realize that Satan will do everything he can to prevent him from going. He should try not to allow self-consciousness or discouragement to rob him of the spirit and the strength to be gained at Church. Whether he knows it or not, part of the pain the excommunicant feels is the effect of the spirit crying for nourishment. That is part of the longing which he has felt, but perhaps, has not understood. One of the most important things he can do is to be in his place every Sunday and, as he attends, to plead for the touch of God's Spirit to soften his heart and to firm his resolve.

XIII
Buffeted

WHEN A PERSON is excommunicated as a result of violating sacred temple covenants, he is not only expelled from the membership of Christ's Church, he is also delivered over to "the buffetings of Satan."

> Therefore, inasmuch as you are found transgressors, you cannot escape my wrath in your lives.
>
> Inasmuch as ye are cut off for transgression, ye cannot escape the buffetings of Satan until the day of redemption.
>
> And I now give unto you power from this very hour, that if any man among you . . . is found a transgressor and repenteth not of the evil, that ye shall deliver him over unto the buffetings of Satan . . . (D&C 104:8-10. See also 78:12; 82:21; 132:26.)

What does this awesome warning mean? I do not believe that anyone can completely explain or describe this horrible experience, but the following is the best definition I have found:

> To be turned over to the *buffetings of Satan* is to be given into his hands; it is to be turned over to him with all the protective power of the priesthood, of righteousness, and of godliness removed, *so that Lucifer is free to torment, persecute, and afflict such a person without let or hindrance.* When the bars are down, the cuffs and curses of Satan, both in this world and in the world to come, bring indescribable anguish

typified by burning fire and brimstone. The damned in
hell so suffer. (Bruce R. McConkie, *Mormon Doctrine,*
2nd Ed., Salt Lake City, Utah: Bookcraft, Inc., 1966,
p. 108; first emphasis is original; second emphasis
added.)

I suppose that these are merely words to a person who
has never suffered through this type of experience, but these
words send shivers of fear down my spine just remembering
what the buffetings were like. Webster's Dictionary of
Synonyms identifies the word "buffet" with other vindictive
words such as beat, pound, pummel, thrash, thresh, baste,
and belabor. A former President of the Church described the
"buffetings of Satan" in these words:

. . . to be turned over to the buffetings of Satan
unto the day of redemption . . . must be something horrible in its nature. Who wishes to endure such torment?
No one but a fool! *I have seen their anguish. I have
heard their pleadings for relief and their pitiful cries
that they cannot endure the torment.* (Joseph Fielding
Smith, *Doctrines of Salvation,* Compiled by Bruce R.
McConkie, 6th Ed., Salt Lake City, Utah: Bookcraft,
Inc., Vol. II, p. 97; emphasis added.)

Many prophets have tried to describe the torment
caused by Satan's "buffetings" by likening it to the agony of
being placed in a lake of "fire and brimstone." (See 2 Ne.
9:19, 26 and Jacob 6:10, for example.) Others have tried to
describe this terrible experience by likening it to having "fiery
darts" thrown at our bodies (see Eph. 6:16; 1 Ne. 15:24;
D&C 27:17.) or to the overpowering force of "whirlwinds,"
"hail," and "mighty storms" beating upon us. (See Alma
26:6; Hel. 5:12.) Still others have referred to the devastating
effect of Satan's buffetings as being held captive in a "gulf of
misery and endless wo." (See 2 Ne. 1:13; Hel. 3:29; 5:12.)
Each of these attempts to describe Satan's buffetings provide
the reader with a tiny glimpse of what it is like to be in
Satan's power. I will attempt to add my own view.

During the two black years which followed my trial, I
was much like a puppet under the control of Satan's
influence. Whenever his hosts of evil spirits felt the need of

some entertainment, they could pull my strings and know that I would perform according to their will. From time to time I was inflicted with the most horrible emotions with no discernable cause. When these ferocious attacks came upon me, I would change in just a few seconds from normal rationality to a nearly insane rage of bitterness and poison which was so overwhelming that it almost choked me. Being so suddenly filled with incomprehensible darkness and evil emotions, and not understanding the source of the feelings, I would find myself lashing out with this vicious venom upon whoever was near, which was usually my family, and most often my wife. I now understand that my suffering was the result of the torment of evil demons who constantly surrounded and taunted me (See Hel. 13:37.), but I did not understand it then.

When this evil influence took possession of me, it was almost as if I could stand beside myself in the same room and observe what was happening — as if I were another person. It was as if I were allowed to stand there and watch this awful behavior as part of my punishment. The Holy Spirit seemed to whisper: *See what your pride and selfishness and disobedience has brought upon you and your family? Now, can you see that it is wiser to yield yourself unto My will than to become a servant and slave to Satan, your enemy?*

I would marvel at how he (myself) could suddenly act so horribly for no apparent cause. I would shudder in amazement and shame at the way that he (myself) was treating the family. Helplessly, what little was left of my decency would protest that this creature could not be me! *It must be a nightmare! This cannot be happening!* My anguished soul would be crying that I didn't want to be that way. I didn't want to act that way. I didn't want this to happen. Yet, I was helpless to resist, for I knew not how.

Sometimes these attacks would be over in a few hours, but often the raging torment would last for days before wearing off. It's a terrifying experience to find oneself suddenly transformed from a normal "day-to-day" person to one possessed of poison, hate, bitterness, and mental anguish so violent that it seems as if one's brain is churning inside one's skull. It's frightening to discover oneself viciously striking out at the very family one is trying to love and hold onto, especially when one does not want to do it but does not know how to stop.

I had absolutely no idea why or how this was happening. It never occurred to me that what I was suffering was part of my punishment, that it was part of the penalty, part of the painful learning experience which I had demanded by my disobedience. I didn't realize that I was constantly "surrounded by demons" as described in Helaman 13:37 and Doctrine and Covenants 76:29. I didn't know that these evil spirits could speak directly to my spirit and thereby cause thoughts and feelings to form "out of nowhere" in my conscious mind. (See 2 Ne. 28:22.) All I knew was that I hurt and that I was hurting everyone around me. I felt the kindest thing I could do would be to disappear from their lives. I knew that I didn't know how to change. I just wanted to die, to cease to exist.

This awful vulnerability to Satan's buffetings hung over me like a constant dark cloud for over two years. Feeling like a rubber band stretched to the breaking point, my emotions were constantly tensed, just waiting and wondering when the next attack would come. I might go for several weeks without a spell, and then suddenly, like a whirlwind and without warning, Satan would invade and occupy again.

I know that I have not described this experience adequately, but these are the only words I can use to describe it. I have failed to communicate the awful horror which we experienced, and my heart aches for the thousands of families who are now groping their way through their buffetings in blindness as we did. I must conclude that the true feelings of such experiences are reserved for those, who, by their improper choices, place themselves in the sad condition of firsthand exposure. To the rest it will remain an experience which they will never fathom. I only hope that what I have tried to describe will help the reader to have compassion and understanding with those who are suffering through it. I plead with you, be kind and patient. Try to reflect the unwavering and unconditional love of the Lord for this person. This is the only way you will be able to endure your own part in such an experience, and your positive reaction and love may be the only light the excommunicated person can find in his penalty of darkness.

That my family could stand by me and continue to believe in me when I was in such an awful state of mind and spirit is a miracle for which I thank my Heavenly Father. The unbelievable constancy of my family's belief and their patient support of me even in the face of my verbal abuses, beamed brightly as evidence of God's love for me. How many times? I cannot count the number of times when their love and patience was all that I had to cling to.

XIV
The Endowment

A GREAT PUZZLE of my excommunication experience was my wife's complete and total forgiveness. I fully expected her to expel me from the home and family. I was almost positive that she would seek a divorce. Yet she forgave, willingly and freely. It was so Christ-like. How could she do that from the very depths of her sorrow?

Another puzzle was how she could endure the insufferable way that I treated the family during those two horrible years when my emotions were under Satanic influence. No one in their right mind would endure what she endured. I totally deserved to be rejected. No one could have criticized or condemned her for insisting that I leave the home when my presence was so evil and depressing. Yet she bore the multitude of injustices which I imposed upon her and the children patiently and kindly, almost passively. Her response to me was like the silent, submissive attitude of the Savior as He allowed the Jews and Romans to heap indignity after indignity upon Him. How could He allow it? How could my wife endure her suffering without protesting and fighting back? How could she continue to believe in me when I was so despicable and when there was not the slightest clue that I would ever improve?

The answers to these questions are of great importance to all who are facing the stress of a similar situation. The truth of the matter is that, on her own, my wife was not able to react in this manner. She couldn't have. No one could! The truth is that she was blessed and endowed through the grace of God with the ability to treat me as He, Himself, would treat me. Because her desire to be in harmony with the Lord's will was paramount in her heart, the Lord actually loaned her the ability to feel and act as He would want her to act!

When I finally escaped from the clutches of Satan's power, I found that the Lord had been there with me through the entire experience, even though I was unaware of it at the time. Part of His influence was manifest in the form of this endowment to my wife of the special ability to work with me and help me find the way back. I know that this is true because I have found the promise in the scriptures and in the personal witness of the Holy Ghost. And I know it because it was specifically revealed to my wife, as will be shown in a moment by a quote from her journal.

Following the court, at the beginning, my wife and I were very unsure of each other. We were more like strangers to each other than when we were first married! We felt very insecure. There were no established boundaries upon our relationship. Each disagreement seemed to blow up all out of proportion. We were both confused. I felt like I was not good enough for her. It seemed that the task of winning her confidence and love back was going to be too hard for me.

Not knowing any other way to cope, our first attempt to deal with the stress of this fragile situation was to merely occupy the same house while allowing no need or trust to exist between us. (Such a precarious coexistence would remind one of the "cold war" relationship between America and Russia.) This, of course, solved nothing. Trying to live together while ignoring each other was a foolish form of retreat which destroyed rather than built our relationship. There was no way that our wounds could heal under that tense condition. With such an impenetrable defensive shield between us, and without tolerance and understanding, neither of us was able to give or receive the love which our marriage needed to survive. How fortunate, then, that the Lord provided a solution to our problem by blessing my wife with the ability to borrow His love and patience and forgiveness. Why would He do such a thing? The answer to this question provides a great testimony of His personal love for each one of us. I believe He did it for four reasons.

First, He loved my wife and wanted to shield her from my verbal abuses and poisonous influence. My deliberate disobedience to His law required me to suffer so that I might find my way to repentance, but she deserved a buffer—a sustaining strength to endure a trial that would quickly surpass her natural strength.

Second, He loved my family and wanted it preserved. He knew that Satan would easily destroy our family without His divine influence to shield them and preserve them until He could effect a cure for my spiritual problems.

Third, He loved me. He knew the hell I was going through. He knew that I could never survive it without the patience and sustaining support of my family. He did it to create an environment in which I could endure my buffetings until I discovered His love.

Fourth, He did this for us because He is who He is and because He is what He is. He did this because He could not sit by and idly watch Satan destroy me. He gave my wife this endowment because He will never do less than all that He can do. He did it because the parables of the Lost Sheep, the Prodigal Son, the Lost Coin are all true representations of His love and ministry and because He never stops seeking that which is lost. His stubborn love will never allow Him to cease from doing all within His power to redeem each soul that is lost.

An excommunication from the Church is not an excommunication from God's love. As God of the entire universe, His perfect love is not limited to Church members. As Paul stated so beautifully, absolutely nothing "shall be able to separate us from the love of God, which is in Christ Jesus our Lord." Not even our sins! (See Rom. 8:35-39.) If it is possible for us to experience an increase of His love and attention at one particular time in our lives, then perhaps His greatest work on our behalf occurs when we are lost and struggling to return. I have learned that He has a very special love for those who are attempting to work their way out of sin.

As I began to yield my life to the Lord, as I began to repent and conquer Satan's influence in my life, a major part of that repentance required that I establish proper relationships with my wife and children. My emotions and affections had to be transformed from the former feelings of resentment and indifference to feelings of appreciation and genuine love and interest.

Ending an excommunication is not so simple as merely refraining from the specific transgression which led to the court. It is, rather, a process of correcting many other faults which have formed barriers between the person and the Lord. I am talking about faults such as my improper feelings towards my family. I am talking about the exchange of hate, envy, grudges, bitterness and malice for the sweet peace of forgiveness, tolerance, respect, and love. I am talking about the exchange of selfishness and preoccupation with self for an interest in the happiness and well-being of others. Working out of an excommunication has nothing to do with Band-aids or aspirins or simply putting a new patch on the tear in the old cloth. It is major surgery. The result must be a total overhaul. Coming back from an excommunication requires going inside of ourselves and casting out everything that is rotten and unworthy of a member of the Lord's Church in exchange for the virtues that lead us towards the Lord. Until we are willing to allow the Lord to perform that total overhaul in us, we are not ready even to consider rebaptism. We are still locked in pride and rebellion, far from the required humility of a "broken heart and contrite spirit."

And so, as I have mentioned, part of my overhaul was

building new skills to love and honor my wife. For the first several months of my conversion, this process progressed wonderfully. We became great friends. We enjoyed being together. We trusted each other. We were very encouraged by our progress.

Then, suddenly, the harmony disappeared. Poof! Like someone had thrown a switch, it was gone! Suddenly trivial things that had been there all along became stumbling blocks. Suddenly my wife was easily offended. She would lose patience with me over little things. After holding on and being so wonderful during those two long years of black hell, now, when I was at my best, she suddenly fell apart. She was overwhelmed and depressed. She seemed to have lost her ability to cope with even the smallest stress.

She was at a total loss to explain her attitude and touchiness. We were both alarmed at what was happening between us. I could see divorce, like an ugly monster, raising its head on the horizon again, but knew not the cause of our problems nor the cure. This new problem so affected my wife that she grew listless and unorganized. The following revelation is taken from her journal entry:

> I had entered a period of depression unlike any I had ever experienced before. It was really awful. For about two weeks all I could do was lie on the couch and brood and wonder what I should be doing. I couldn't even organize my thoughts or formulate any plans for keeping house, etc.
>
> Finally I got on my knees and asked the Lord, "WHY? What was happening to me?" As I pled for understanding, it was given to me. I was told that all through the trials and adversity of my husband's excommunication and subsequent buffeting by Satan I had been given extra help from beyond the veil; strength and power to endure that were more than my own ability.
>
> I was told that now that the Lord had healed him the endowment was no longer proper. Now it was up to me to learn to adjust and to grow with him — to improve myself along with him. I was told that the "extra"

help had been withdrawn from me, and now I needed to re-adjust and gain control and strength through my own efforts, with the continued help of the Lord, of course.

It overwhelmed me when that aid was first withdrawn, but after the Lord was merciful and kind enough to give me the explanation, I was able to work my way out of it all. Now I believe I've come to the point where we are working together in harmony and love and concern for each other as the Lord intended. And I feel he has taken his rightful place at my head and I am so much more content and happy to be at his heart and not the leader.

Again I testify to the reader who is fighting to survive the stress of broken or threatened relationships that one does not have to bear such experiences alone. The Lord desires and asks for our permission to be a part of our afflictions. He yearns to reach out and strengthen, comfort, and sustain us in the time of our greatest need. (See D&C 133:53; Heb. 4:15-16; Matt. 11:28-29, for example.) Don't insist on carrying the cross alone. Even the Savior had to have help with His cross. Allow Him to help with yours. Allow the Lord to help you manifest His love for the one you are trying to support by yielding your burdens to Him so that He may strengthen your abilities.

I know that when we finally trust Him enough to release our yoke and our burdens to Him, we open the door to receive His grace which He promised would always be "sufficient" to solve our problems. (See Philip. 4:19; 2 Cor. 9:8; Ether 12:26; D&C 17:8; 18:31.) I have shown how the Lord bestowed an endowment of His grace upon my wife. He has assured us that He never changes. The scriptures teach that what He does for one He is willing to do for all who will allow it. The first principle of the Gospel is faith in Jesus Christ. A major part of that faith is allowing Him to perform the work in us and through us which we are incapable of doing on our own.

XV
Glimpses of the Children

MY CHILDREN ENDURED untold suffering because of my behavior. My suffering was just; it was my own fault, but they certainly did not deserve the contentious spirit and frustrations which I inflicted upon them. What an awful price the family pays from the apostacy of a loved one. Two events may reveal some of what they endured.

Shortly after a heated exchange of criticism between my wife and me which was in the hearing of some of our children, I found one of my teenage daughters sitting at the desk in my den writing a letter. She looked so pained and desperate that, in spite of my personal frustrations, I couldn't help but put my hand on her shoulder and ask what was wrong. She immediately broke into heartrending sobs. Nothing I say can better portray the hardship placed upon the children during the "buffeting period" of the excommunication than the words of her letter.

> Dear Grandma,
>
> Things have been going so rotten. If only you were here everything would seem to be okay. Mom and Dad—when they get into fights, it really makes me cry. I am writing this while they are mad at each other.
>
> Right now I feel like bursting out yelling all of my problems instead of holding them deep within myself. I just can't seem to go talk to my parents anymore. If only you were here so I could talk with you.

Oh, Grandma, I pray and pray and pray for them,
but nothing seems to work. What should I do?

My guilty heart was cut to the quick. For a moment I was able to see the family's torment clearer than my own, and I promised her that I would try to do better. I really meant it, but none of my promises lasted very long in those dark days. I am sure that the prayers of this broken-hearted girl and the other children had a lot to do with the wonderful endowment of patience which was subsequently given to my wife.

There was another event which also cut my conscience to the quick. Our home had one upstairs bedroom used by three of our daughters. Because I worked the night shift, I would sleep up there during the day where I could be away from the family noise. During the awful period when I had abandoned myself to pornography without restraint, I had a terrible dream about my nine-year-old daughter whose bed I used.

I dreamed that I had slipped over the edge of a precipice of a very deep chasm. As I was clinging to the cliff, this nine-year-old daughter came running to help me. But she also slipped and fell past me into the chasm towards certain death. In dumb-founded terror I screamed her name as I helplessly watched her fall. As her body fell further and further from my sight, I could hear her calling to me, "I love you, Dad . . . I love you, Dad."

I awoke from the dream in a cold sweat. I could not go back to sleep. That the dream had meaning, I was certain, but what could it mean? Were we going to lose her with a premature death? Was she going to fall away from the Church as I had? The meaning of the dream was made plain to me when I told my wife about it. She pointed out that my daughter's fall was related to my fall. If I had not been in jeopardy, she would not have perished. My wife then confided to me that for some time this young daughter had complained of feeling evil spirits who were "putting bad thoughts" in her mind, especially when she was trying to go to sleep. Among other things, they told her not to pray, not to read the scriptures, and not to believe her teachers at church. The torment was so persistent, and she was so often frightened that she frequently had to leave her bed and join my wife in our bedroom to feel safe again. Often she was awakened by terrifying dreams.

The bond between her peril and mine was obvious when I realized that the evil influence of my lust and pornographic fantasies lingered not only in the room where I slept, but most particularly with that bed which we shared. No doubt there were many evil spirits who frequented this bedroom to take vicarious pleasure in watching my self-abuse. While I was gone, they busied themselves tormenting her.

Truly, no person can claim that the effect of their sin is limited to their own life! We cannot hide what we are from our loved ones. Nor can we hide the influence of our secret desires. I was able to feel a sorrow for my daughter that I could not feel for myself. I never used her bed again, and after she received a priesthood blessing, she was no longer troubled by the evil spirits. How I envied her blessing. I knew that it would protect her, but I also knew that in my wickedness I was beyond protection. I still had much to learn before I would turn towards the Master.

About three weeks before he was to leave for his mission, my oldest son came home from BYU. By this time, I had been swept back into the enslavement of pornography for some time. I had tried to resist and failed so many times that I had totally given up. I felt that I was now ready for suicide or any escape I could find. None of my children knew about my addiction to pornography. Thus, you can imagine this sweet boy's shock as he was looking through my den for some genealogy records and discovered my hidden briefcase full of pornographic magazines.

This sweet spiritual boy who had kept himself pure and innocent for nineteen years, how crushed he must have been. And yet, he never once allowed this terrible discovery to isolate him from me. Rather, he began to pour out his love and support upon me. Refusing to accept my failures as permanent, he launched a "change Dad's attitude" campaign. All over the house he began taping 3 × 5 cards— on my mirror, on the bedroom door, in the stairway, on the refrigerator, etc. The following are some of the things he wrote:

> "You were sent here to succeed, and YOU WILL."
>
> "I believe in you!"
>
> "You *CAN* do it, you will do it, you *ARE* doing it!"
>
> "Dad, I love you! You are the GREATEST, and I would not trade you for anyone or anything. You are a good man; please begin to believe it."
>
> "You can't be too bad with a wife, two sons, six daughters, two sets of parents, brothers and sisters loving you, respecting you, praying for you, wanting you to succeed, wishing they could help you, knowing how good you are."
>
> "You get points just for hanging on. (I thought about this one a lot and still do.) Congratulate yourself and keep it up. Endure in faith to the end."
>
> "With so many other people convinced you are worth loving and forgiving, why can't you love and forgive yourself?"
>
> "Forgive yourself 70 × 7. Start now. Think of the past 490 things you've done wrong and forgive yourself of them, bad as they may be. Let yourself be the good man you really are."

What a remarkably forgiving attitude he had, when he could have been so easily crushed by disappointment in me. He really made me want to try again.

If the reader is part of an excommunicated person's family, please know how desperately that person needs you to believe in him, especially when he can't believe in himself. Help him to lean on your faith. Don't nag or criticize. His conscience is so tender. Give him the benefit of the doubt. Allow him to make mistakes. He is probably not capable of living up to the standards at the beginning, and may never be unless you believe in him. Let him feel that you are going to stand with him no matter how long it takes. How much chance will he have if the family or the spouse grows impatient and gives up on him? What he needs most of all is patience and love and the Lord. But he may never find Him if those closest to him allow bitterness and impatience to dominate the relationship. How long does God expect us to forgive? When do we have the right to abandon one who has gone astray? These are hard questions. The Holy Ghost will provide the needed inspiration for your specific situation when sought prayerfully in a submissive attitude.

How grateful I am that of my family—my wife, my children, my parents, my brothers and sisters, my in-laws, my Bishop, and Home Teacher—not one of them ever gave up on me. Please remember that "those who need love the most usually deserve it the least." Learn to see the bitterness and frustrations of the excommunicated person for what they really are, an unspoken plea for love and self-worth.

XVI
The War Is Not Over

ABOUT A YEAR and a half after my excommunication, my wife and children attended her family reunion. Because of my job, I was not able to attend, nor would I have wanted to if I could. I didn't want to be around anyone, especially happy people, and her family was always happy! At that reunion her family decided to fast weekly and pray on my behalf. It really made a difference! My heart began to soften. My resolves and determination were strengthened. Bitterness began to recede, and new hope came into my life. My thinking became clearer, and I began to discover things about myself that I had never known. Several weeks later, my wife revealed to me that her family had been fasting and praying for me. I was surprised and moved by their compassion and concern, but what amazed me the most was the effect it had upon me. The total effect of their weeks of fasting on my behalf was so profound that I sent a copy of the following letter to each of them in appreciation:

> Dear Family,
>
> I want to thank you for your fasting and prayers and trust and patient support. When my wife told me of your plan to fast, I was quite surprised and moved. But most important is the wonderful effect it has had on me. This is the first time I have ever felt or recognized a direct and tangible benefit from the prayers of others, and it is wonderful.

I feel a tremendous change in my attitudes and perception of my problems. It seems I have been stumbling in the dark and didn't know it. The things that I thought were my main problems and on which I focused all of my attentions were more the symptoms than the cause. In the last few weeks I have become aware of many other areas in my character and personality that are crying for change and improvement.

> And if any man shall seek to build up himself, and seeketh not my counsel, *HE SHALL HAVE NO POWER,* and his folly shall be made manifest. (D&C 136:19; emphasis added. See also D&C 3:4.)

Well, I think that at last I can see my folly and reason for lack of power. I have been trying to analyze myself, diagnose myself and cure myself. What pride! What stupidity! What blindness! I feel humbled and ashamed to finally realize that I have tried to reach heaven by my own merits and good works alone. It's true we need to obey and qualify ourselves as best we can, but "it is by grace that we are saved, after all we can do." (2 Ne. 25:23.)

I am ashamed of the time I have wasted blundering around on my own, and of the offense it must be to the Lord. But I am also excited because, even though I have failed to appreciate the Savior's sacrifice on my behalf, I now see the direction I must go and can now feel hope of success because of doing it His way through His powers.

I am also ashamed of the years I have wasted for my wife. I can see now what a wonderful treasure she is and how ungrateful I have been for her. How much I have taken for granted. While it is presently difficult for me to conceive of the reality of the Lord's love and forgiveness to me, I can glimpse it through my wife for she has been so kind, loyal, patient and forgiving to me that my heart swells in gratitude. I desire to reward her with an honorable life worthy of that favor she has bestowed on me.

I see now that I have much to learn and much to do, yet I feel so helpless for I am walking into paths hitherto unknown to me. I thank you for your support and appreciate a continuation of your prayers. You are a wonderful family, and I am thankful my wife and children are part of your heritage. I promise to strive for worthiness to be part of you.

I know it will take considerable time for me to learn the necessary lessons and develop the proper habits of attitude and performance, but I no longer feel hopeless and defeated. I now have a new confidence and sense of direction. I hope and pray that I have permanently escaped the curse of wavering vacillation and can keep my feet firmly on the path forwards towards the Lord.

Thank you and my love,
Steven

One can see from this letter that my thoughts and emotions were turning in the right direction—away from my own limitations and towards the grace and power of the Lord. I had, at last, caught a glimpse of the real solution to my problems. But the war was far from over. Satan took this letter as a warning sign that I was slipping from his grasp, and, surrounding me with evil spirits, he launched an overwhelming attack that drove me right back into the jaws of the filthy hell that had become so familiar. Like a toothpick before a bulldozer, I crumbled before his invasion. In less than four months I fell from the spiritual height of this letter to the rock-bottom depths of darkness and despair. I fell to the point that I was ready to try drugs, alcohol, suicide—anything to escape the pain of having to live with myself and my failure. I was totally defeated. I stumbled through constant darkness and confusion. I had given up. I would try only once more. I prepared myself for one last desperate attempt and then total destruction. I knew I was drowning, and I knew I was going down for the last time.

XVII
Surrender At Last

NO ONE CAN hope to escape from their faults and failures until they are willing to face what they have become in total brutal honesty. I finally reached that point at Christmas, almost two years after my excommunication. At last I was able to see myself for what I really was: a filthy slave to my carnal nature, an addict to pornography and self-love, a failure with my family and myself, a hopeless, hollow and helpless wretch, a totally miserable creature who hated himself so much that he would prefer not to exist.

I could not go on with life. There was no way I would endure another year like the last two. I had endured to the limit. As a "last-ditch effort," I went for a long walk along a river where I could be alone and pray. There was no faith or confidence in my prayer. It was not a petition of faith to a loving Heavenly Father, but more like a condemned man's bewildered plea for mercy. I knew that I had exhausted my own resources. I was completely wrung dry. There was no more fight left in me. I knew that I was totally in Satan's power, and I felt completely helpless to escape. I was carried about by Satan's desires as helplessly as a twig in a raging torrent. I had been beaten down so many times that I felt like a bloody pulp at the bottom of a thousand-foot well. I finally recognized that there was absolutely no possibility of escape on my own power, from what I had become.

I finally realized that I had nowhere else to turn but to the Lord. (How stubborn I was to resist such a simple lesson.) I walked and prayed for a long time. I told Heavenly Father how hard I had tried to love him; I told Him how hard I had tried to love my wife and children; how hard I had tried to overcome my faults; how hard I had tried to forgive myself. But my efforts had failed. I was losing ground. I was further away from Him and the Church now than I was when I was excommunicated. My feeble attempts to come closer to Him were constantly washed away by the tidal wave of hate and guilt that I felt for myself. How could I ever love someone else when I was so full of hate for my own failure? At last I admitted to Him (and myself) that I was absolutely powerless to save myself. I finally recognized and admitted that, unless He reached out to save me, I would be lost forever. They were bitter words, but at last I was admitting that I needed a Savior. I could not do it by myself. At last I could see that I could never make myself good enough for God without His help. I admitted that, if He saw fit to rescue me, it would require pure mercy; for, I had absolutely no merit upon which to base my plea.

The heavens seemed silent. I felt no peace nor assurance that my request was heard, and I continued groping awkwardly with no real hope of response. My prayer was like a drowning man's involuntary cry for help even though he knows there is no one within miles to hear his plea.

I fasted that day and the next in an effort to show God I really meant what I said. I wanted Him to know that I knew that I was literally at the end of my rope and had no more strength to hang on. This was the end. My life was now in His hands. Either He would do something, or I would perish, surrendering myself forever to the victorious Lucifer.

My stubborn pride and insistence upon fixing myself up all by myself finally crumbled. At last I got myself out of the Lord's way and opened the door to Him. At last I gave Him the opportunity to demonstrate His power to heal, where my own power had failed so miserably. At last my pitiful life was ready to turn. My descent had ended. I was about to discover Jesus Christ and the power of His Atonement, and, in discovering the reality of His personal love for me, I would discover the real me that He and my Heavenly Father had loved all along—the "me" that was so submerged in filth that it was unknown even to myself—the real me that had been struggling for identity and freedom all those long, long years—the part of me that still cared. All the rest of me was soon to die, soon to be crucified and buried through the power of the Atonement, making way for spiritual birth and love for Heavenly Father and the Savior of mankind, my Elder Brother who had loved me through it all.

XVIII
Rescued

AFTER GROPING MY way through that "last-chance prayer" along the river, I came away bitterly disappointed. Though I had absolutely no conception of what God could do for me, or how He might answer my prayer, in my rock-bottom desperation I had gone crawling to Him. But He hadn't seemed to answer. Why didn't He care anymore? I would soon learn that He had heard my cry for help just as He hears and answers every sincere prayer. I would soon learn that He cared for my plight just as He cares for the suffering of every one of His children. The immutable promise of God is that ALL who sincerely ask, "with real intent," shall receive.

I received His answer to my prayer within a few days through a talk I heard. The talk was about "the doctrine of Christ." I did not know what that meant. I could not recall ever hearing that expression before (It is mentioned in *The Book of Mormon* over a dozen times!), but as I listened to the speaker, my tormented life came to a screeching halt. The words I heard caused everything else in my world to disappear; for a moment time stood still as I felt and heard the Spirit saying to me, "THIS IS THE ANSWER YOU HAVE BEEN SEEKING. ONLY IN JESUS CHRIST WILL YOU FIND PEACE AND THE POWER TO HEAL YOUR WOUNDS. HE HAS BEEN WAITING FOR YOU SO

LONG. WHEN WILL YOU OPEN YOUR LIFE TO HIM?" This revelation was as real and certain as if an angel had appeared to me. Through every fiber of my being I sensed that my life had just encountered a turning point and that I would never again be the same.

The speaker's main idea was to point out the division of the gospel into two parts, the vast body of "moral and ethical principles" (meaning all the do's and don'ts, most of which are common to almost every religion) and the "doctrine of Christ," where we find the real power to overcome our faults and become "partakers of the divine nature." (See 2 Pet. 1:4.) He said that using the humanistic approach to overcome our faults and imperfections (in other words, using all of our energy to work on the "moral and ethical principles" alone) could, with sufficient will power and determination, result in the eventual control of our behavior, but would never enable us to qualify for more than a terrestrial glory.

The speaker went on to say that the only power to achieve a celestial life comes through our relationship with the Savior. It is His mission to lift us from the limitations of our mortal weaknesses and sins (our "natural man" or human tendencies) to a celestial level of behavior so that we may, through His atonement, actually have our nature changed and become worthy to return to the Father. He said that it is only by making the Savior the center and foundation of our life that we will ever gain the power to change our human nature and love of evil.[1]

For the first time in my life, I became aware of the difference between controlling human behavior through will power and the actual modification of our human nature through the power of Christ's atonement. I certainly did not understand what this meant, but each time I pondered it, the Spirit would bear witness to me that here, in "the doctrine of

---

[1]George W. Pace, Developing A Personal Relationship With The Savior, Salt Lake City, Utah: Covenant Recordings, Inc., 1979.

Christ," I would find the answer and the power I had been seeking.

All my life I had been tormented by the struggle between the carnal part of me that craved pornography and self-love and the spiritual part of me that wanted to love and obey God. Now at last I could see that through those thirty years I had been struggling to control my behavior, I was only working on the symptom. The real problem was not my behavior, but my human nature, which only the Lord could change.

Turning to the scriptures, I found "the doctrine of Christ" to be a major theme, especially in *The Book of Mormon* which I had read over a dozen times and never understood! (See 2 Ne. chapters 31 and 32; 3 Ne. 11:30-41.) How blind I had been. Everywhere I looked I found the scriptures full of Christ's power to deliver us from our evil nature. Alma described it this way:

> Behold, *he changed their hearts;* yea, he awakened them out of a deep sleep, and they awoke unto God. Behold, they were in the midst of darkness; nevertheless, their souls were illuminated by the light of the everlasting word . . . (Alma 5:7; emphasis added.)

I began to experience this same awakening. I read the testimony of King Benjamin's people concerning his words to them of the Savior:

> Yea, we believe all the words which thou hast spoken unto us; and also, we know of their surety and truth, because of the Spirit of the Lord Omnipotent, *which has wrought a mighty change in us, or in our hearts, that we have no more disposition to do evil, but to do good continually.* (Mosiah 5:2; emphasis added.)

Oh, what a "mighty change" indeed! To think of it, "no more disposition to do evil!" How does it happen? How could I obtain this mighty change in my own heart? I found that they had obtained it by first acknowledging their own utter unworthiness and inability to save themselves. (This I had already recognized in my "last chance" prayer.)

Secondly, they expressed their faith in the Savior and specifically asked God to "apply" the merits of the Savior's blood on their behalf.

> And they had viewed themselves in their own carnal state, even less than the dust of the earth. And they all cried aloud with one voice, saying: *O have mercy, and apply the atoning blood of Christ that we may receive forgiveness of our sins, and our hearts may be purified;* for we believe in Jesus Christ, the Son of God . . . (Mosiah 4:2; emphasis added.)

Could His redemption actually be had for the asking? Certainly it would never be found without asking! How blind and stupid I had been. I had been so busy trying to control my behavior that it never occurred to me to ask Heavenly Father to allow Jesus Christ to change my nature through the power of His Atonement. I read the Savior's own words about our total and absolute dependency upon Him for access to the Father:

> I am the true vine, and my Father is the husbandman.
>
> I am the vine, ye are the branches . . .
>
> Abide in me, and I in you. As the branch cannot bear fruit of itself, except it abide in the vine; no more can ye, except ye abide in me.
>
> If a man abide not in me, he is cast forth as a branch, and is withered . . . (John 15:1, 5, 4, 6. See also 1 Ne. 15:14-15.)

No wonder my life was so frustrated and "withered." I had never been close to the Savior, nor had I dared allow Him to be close to me. In my efforts to reach the Father, I had ignored the Savior. I had never learned to rely upon Him for the strength and power I needed to overcome my faults. I had always believed that I must perfect myself *before* He could accept me. But now I realized that if that were possible, we would not even need a Savior. No man who deserved redemption would need redeeming.

Why hadn't He rescued me and healed me before? He couldn't. Not while I was in the way. I was so busy trying to save myself that I had left no room for His help. And so He had to wait until I realized with all of my being that I was never going to cure myself all by myself. Only then could I open my life to His power.

Not long after receiving this revelation about Christ being the solution to my problems, I found a religious tract which bore a second witness to me of my need for the Savior. It said:

> *Every religion in the world, except Christianity, boils down to an effort by man to attain heaven by climbing a ladder of goodness and working his way to God.* Christianity is unique. The gospel of Jesus stands alone. It alone is a record of God's coming down to man, His condescension in Jesus Christ to provide for man what man could not do for himself.
>
> The scriptures tell us that the wages of sin is death. Because we willingly choose against God—and sin is just that; an attitude of independence from God—the result of our sin is alienation from God, described in the New Testament as spiritual death. *A spiritually dead man cannot bring himself back to life.* (Author unknown; emphasis added.)

As I studied the "doctrine of Christ" I found many witnesses that Jesus Christ is "The Way," indeed, the *only* way for us to become what we need to become to reach the Father. (John 14:6.) I found the following words, for example, in a Gospel Doctrine manual:

> "I am the Way," the Savior tells those who hope to find the means, the way to create heaven. *Only in him can any man find the strength, the power and ability to live a godly life. Only in Christ is there power to transform the human mind and the human heart,* that in a purified state men might attain and enjoy happiness.
>
> It is possible to desire and work for righteousness and heaven in many religions. But only in the restored gospel and Church of Jesus Christ is it possible, is there power, to achieve righteousness and heaven in this world. The Savior is the way, and the only way.
>
> Jesus Christ is the truth. His way to salvation is

based on truth. Only in Jesus Christ can any man learn
the truth of what he is and how he can be changed from
what he is to do the good for which he hopes. (In His
Footsteps Today, Salt Lake City, Utah: Deseret Sunday
School Union, 1969, p. 4; emphasis added.)

If man is to become like Christ, by means of the
Holy Spirit, he must begin to partake of the divine truth
and power which Jesus possesses. *A major purpose of
Christ's mission on earth was to reveal his glory to
man* (John 1:14) *and to give man the divine truth
and power required to attain to salvation in the presence
of God.* (In His Footsteps Today, p. 29; emphasis
added.)

I found a multitude of scriptures and quotations such as
the following which emphasize our absolute dependency
upon the Savior if we are ever to escape our evil nature and
become worthy to reach the Father. Each new scripture
added to my knowledge and faith.

And now, my sons, remember, remember that *it is
upon the rock of our Redeemer, who is Christ, the Son
of God, that ye must build your foundation;* that when
the devil shall send forth his mighty winds, yea, his
shafts in the whirlwind, yea, when all his hail and his
mighty storm shall beat upon you, it shall have no
power over you to drag you down to the gulf of misery
and endless wo, because of the rock upon which ye are
built, *which is a sure foundation, a foundation whereon
if men build they cannot fall.* (Hel. 5:12; emphasis
added.)

I am Messiah, the King of Zion, the Rock of
Heaven, which is broad as eternity; *whoso cometh in at
the gate and climbeth up by me shall never fall* . . .
(Moses 7:53; emphasis added.)

. . . that they might know the promises of the Lord,
and that they may believe the gospel *and rely upon the
merits of Jesus Christ,* and be glorified through faith
in his name . . . (D&C 3:20; emphasis added. See also
2 Ne. 31:19; Moro. 6:4.)

*The greatest and most important of all require-
ments of our Father in Heaven and of his Son Jesus*

Christ . . . is to believe in Jesus Christ, confess him, seek to know him, cling to him, make friends with him. Take a course to open a communication with your Elder Brother or file-leader—our Savior. (Brigham Young, *Journal of Discourses,* Vol. 8, p. 339. Also quoted in *1982 Relief Society Manual,* Salt Lake City, Utah: The Church of Jesus Christ of Latter-day Saints, p. 25; emphasis added.)

We function best in an environment of freedom. We are free when we are independent, and *we are totally independent only when we are completely dependent upon the Savior.* (Hugh W. Pinnock, *Devotional Speeches of the Year,* Provo, Utah: Brigham Young University Press, 1979, p. 116; emphasis added.)

I found dozens of scriptures and quotations such as the following to witness to us that Jesus Christ is both able and willing to lend us the strength we lack so that we may become like Him as we overcome our imperfections through His power and grace. I was really getting excited. For the first time in my life I could see a light of true and permanent victory.

. . . he has all power to save every man that believeth on his name and bringeth forth fruit meet for repentance. (Alma 12:15.)

Yea, I know that I am nothing; as to my strength I am weak; therefore I will not boast of myself, but I will boast of my God, for *in his strength I can do all things* . . . (Alma 26:12; emphasis added.)

He giveth power to the faint; and to them that have no might he increaseth strength. (Isa. 40:29.)

And Christ hath said: If ye will have faith in me ye shall have power to do whatsoever thing is expedient in me. (Moro. 7:33.)

Nevertheless, the Lord God showeth us our weakness that we may know that it is by his grace, and his great condescensions unto the children of men, that we have power to do these things. (Jacob 4:7.)

The gospel is not merely a moral code of living based on seeking to acquire the attributes of the Savior, *but is also the actual means* [power] essential to salva-

tion. (N. Eldon Tanner, *Ensign,* April 1982, p. 5;
emphasis added.)

My escape from Satan's power was not as sudden as
Alma's, who, in the very instant of recognizing Christ in his
life, was relieved of his anguish and filled with unspeakable
joy, peace, and forgiveness. (See Alma 36:1-24.) But my
rescue was just as real and wonderful as his was. Slowly,
purposefully, step-by-step, the Lord began to work the
miracles of His rescue and salvation in my life. Line upon
line, never faster than I could receive it, He began directing
the proper help into my life. He made me aware of truths I
had never recognized before. He began to open scriptures to
my understanding which built my faith in Him. He raised up
friends to help. He awakened me to a life of joy and peace
that I had never in my wildest imaginations thought possible.

As I repented of my previous indifference to the Savior's
sacrifice, and as He worked with me to cast away all that was
unholy, He helped me to understand that I must repent of
many other faults besides my moral transgressions. One
major problem, for example, was the indifference and
resentment I had felt towards my family. He helped me to
discover that our relationship with Heavenly Father is
directly related to our relationship with our family. We
cannot expect to grow close to Him and still maintain
grudges or even casual indifference towards our family. I
could only proceed so far until it became obvious that my
relationship with my wife and family must be healed and set
in proper order before I could grow closer to Him. Learning
to love and appreciate them was a wonderful joy.

As the Lord changed my heart and nature, He also took
away the love of evil and the awful enslavement to pornography and self-love which had dominated my life for over
thirty years. After all those years it was simply gone! In its
place I had a new sense of self-worth and a burning love for
my Savior and my Heavenly Father. I had a miraculous
awareness of Their love for me. I became a totally new
person. At last I was through trying to reach Heavenly

Father by short-cutting around the Savior with my will power and good works alone. At last I had learned that I, like every human being upon this planet, need the Savior.

The Lord changed my life from despair to ecstacy, from lust to love and from helplessness to victory. How one could make such a miraculous journey in just a few months may seem incomprehensible to those who are unfamiliar with His magnificent power; but it did happen.

Paul taught that our faith in Jesus Christ is proportionate to the degree that we are willing to "hear" the word of God about Christ. (See Rom. 10:17.) Because I plunged myself into the scriptures, they became a major factor in my rescue and healing. For a year and a half, I spent every spare minute searching and studying. My faith that the Savior could, in fact, become my Savior grew by leaps and bounds. I typed, word for word, compiled and analyzed over two-thousand references which testify that Jesus Christ is a God of power, love, kindness, patience, and mercy. They testify that He will share with us all that is required to change our natures from the vacillation of the "natural man" to a true man of God. They testify that through surrendering to Him and trusting His will, we can be changed from what we are to what He would have us be. They testify that He came to rescue us FROM our sins, not to sit idly by, waiting until we have somehow cleansed and delivered ourselves. He is truly THE WAY out of our sins, and He is THE ONLY WAY back to the Father.

I am not suggesting that such an exhaustive study is required of every person. Certainly it would benefit all who are willing to pay that price, but I am only sharing what I did. I was so ignorant of the Savior's grace, and I was so blind to His love and power and interest in me that such a study was invaluable in building my faith and confidence to reach out to Him. As my faith in the Savior grew, I was at last able to feel the Father's love and concern for me. The more that I learned of Them, the more astonished I grew. I was embarking on a wonderfully exciting adventure!

Another important part of my rescue came through the loving influence of a new friend. Because of my moral transgressions, I had felt inferior, hollow, and hypocritical all of my life. Consequently, I had never had even one close friend. I had never allowed anyone, including my own wife, to know me well. I kept everyone at a distance, most of all the Lord. With my intellect I knew that God must love me. He had to because "God is love." But, in my heart, and with my emotions, I simply could not conceive of a love so great that it could see past my faults to my needs. The only love I had ever understood was conditional love, offered when worthy, withdrawn when unworthy.

I have a testimony that when we are ready, God will raise up the right kind of friends who can speak for Him and help to lead us to Him. My new friend worked in the Church Seminary program and had a great deal of counselling experience. His friendship was invaluable. He befriended me with an unconditional love, without criticism or judgement for what I had done or for what I had become. Like the Lord, he believed I could change. My friend spent time with me when I needed to talk. I knew that I was free to call him anytime of the day or night. I could tell him anything— my fears, my worries and doubts, my sins. Along with my scripture study, my friend helped me to discover and trust in the Lord's unwavering love for me. I emphasize this part of my rescue in the hope that every excommunicant will find a kind Home Teacher, a Priesthood leader, or someone who will care enough to stick with him for as long as it takes to work his way back. Nothing is as powerful as love!

My friend taught me to let go of my terrible past by allowing the Savior to heal my present. (He can't fix today if all we think about is yesterday.) He also taught me from the scriptures that we have no right to judge, condemn or punish ourselves for our sins or weaknesses. Judgement and punishment belong to God, not to man. Together we discovered that I had actually allowed my feelings of guilt to become a form of self-punishment for my cycles of sin. We discovered that in a perverted sort of way, I was substituting self-imposed misery for true repentance. He also taught me that letting go of our grudges, letting go of our bitterness and malice, particularly that which we feel towards ourselves, is a necessary part of placing our faith in the Savior's atonement.

Thus, the third part of my rescue and spiritual healing came from learning to finally "let go" or release my guilt, my burdens, and my self-condemnation to the Lord. Call it "yielding" or "surrendering" or "submitting" ourselves; call it what you will, we must not only yield our will to His in terms of obedience, but we must also surrender to Him our very sins, our faults, our bad habits, weaknesses, hurts, fears, doubts—everything which is rotten and unworthy of one who belongs to Him. As President Kimball has said:

> When a defiled man is born again, his habits are changed, his thoughts cleansed, his attitudes regenerated and elevated, his activities put in total order, and everything about him that was dirty, degenerate or reprobate is washed and made clean. (*Miracle of Forgiveness,* 1st Ed., Salt Lake City, Utah: Bookcraft, Inc., 1969, p. 352.)

As I came to understand this principle, I went before the Lord and admitted the terrible mess I had made of my life. I confessed that I finally knew that I was not capable of guiding my own life. I confessed my realization that I could not live a pure and holy life without His power to change me. I surrendered everything to Him—my life, my will, my agency, my future, my time, my energy, even my faults and imperfections. I gave Him everything that I am or ever could be and covenanted to live for Him and like Him. Then I reviewed my life. Starting with my worst sins, the adultery, the pornography, and self-stimulation, I began confessing. I verbally identified and described every deliberate sin I could remember and surrendered each of them, asking Him to apply the Savior's atonement to free me from them. I said something like this:

> Father in Heaven, I surrender this sin. I am sorry I ever did it. I no longer claim it as mine. I reject it. I

give it up along with all that it involves. I surrender it to
thee and plead for thee to remove it from my life; for,
by myself, I am weak and prone to sin. I plead with thee
to give me the strength to cast it from my life and to live
worthy of thy presence and power from this point
forward. I plead with thee to apply the Savior's atonement on my behalf that I may become pure and worthy
before thee. I thank thee for the atonement and for thy
love and mercy in showing me the way back.

When our surrender is given sincerely and from the
heart, this process of giving up our sins and burdens becomes
a very real personal experience. This is the actual giving up
or transferring of the sin, and everything associated with it,
to Jesus Christ. I am not implying that all who need to
unburden themselves of sin should do so in this exact
manner, but it was effective for me. In all things, we should
let the Spirit be our guide. But this wonderful process is part
of what it took to break the pride and stubbornness in my
heart and make my spirit more contrite, soft, and yielding to
the Spirit.

This experience was so real to me that it was almost
tangible. I could actually feel myself being cleansed. I could
feel His peace and acceptance flowing into my soul. It was so
real that it almost seemed as if I were kneeling at the feet of
my Heavenly Father and the Savior, and They were saying to
me, "We have been waiting such a long time for you to share
these burdens with Us. We are so glad that at last you have
decided to believe Us and to trust Us and to come to Us so
that We may do for you all that We have promised to do for
each man's salvation."

What I have described was a process, not a single event.
I had to go through these surrendering sessions for several
months as other sins came to mind which I had forgotten.
Each bit of poison thusly surrendered made my load lighter
and increased my love for Heavenly Father and the Savior.

I do not have the words to describe the intensity of the
love and gratitude which I now feel for my Savior, and which
I have received from Him and Heavenly Father. I have

learned that Their divine and stubborn love simply cannot be reduced to the confinement of mortal words. Truly, Their love "passeth knowledge," but it does not pass the understanding and perception of our experience. Personal experience is the only way we can ever begin to conceive of Their infinite love for us.

Some have said, "You make too much of it. You exaggerate. You have built it all out of proportion. There is no way possible that God could feel so much and care so much about each individual when there are so many."

In response to this mistaken belief I feel that we can scarcely imagine a millionth of all that Their love for us really is. I know Their great love, for I have felt it. It has healed me. I cannot describe it, I cannot justify it, but I know that I will spend the rest of my life trying to reflect it into the lives of others.

I know that what I have described in this chapter is true. I testify to all who are enslaved by bad habits, by sins, by weaknesses, and addictions that Jesus Christ is a God of power. No matter what the problem is, He is "The Way" out of it. The Savior's intervention in my life was an act of total mercy, for I had absolutely no merit with which to claim His blessings. We cannot buy His mercy. He is both able and anxious to bless each of us with a power and grace that can lift our nature far above the limitations of our own human abilities. He does this that He may share with us the love and fellowship which He enjoys with the Father. The Lord does not change, nor is He a respecter of persons; therefore, the fact that He did this for me is evidence that He is willing to do it for all who will accept it.

On the cross, our Savior declared: "It is finished!" He was proclaiming that the atonement was prepared and ready for man's release. The work of the atonement is not "finished," however, until it is accepted in our own heart. I urge every person to open their heart to Him.

> For we have not an high priest which cannot be
> touched with the feeling of our infirmities; but was

in all points tempted like as we are, yet without sin.

Let us therefore come boldly unto the throne of grace, that we may obtain mercy, and find grace to help in time of need. (Heb. 4:15-16.)

Behold, I stand at the door, and knock: if any man hear my voice, and open the door, I will come in to him . . . (Rev. 3:20.)

XIX
Baptism

BEFORE AN EXCOMMUNICATED person can be rebaptized, he must go before a court of the same stake High Council or Bishopric before which he was excommunicated. These men must be satisfied by the evidence presented, and by inspiration, that the person has truly repented and has become worthy of rebaptism. When I was certain I had been healed of my spiritual problems, when healthy relationships had been established with my family, and when I felt that I had been forgiven, I called for an appointment with our Stake President.

Once the appointment was made, there were several weeks to wait. During this waiting period, we made it a matter of every family prayer that the Stake President's response to the interview would be favorable. Then, on the evening of the interview, we had a wonderful spiritual experience. After a period of fasting, my wife and I gathered the family together and had a discussion about repentance and making amends, about paying the required price for our mistakes and about forgiveness. We emphasized the truth that God is in charge and guides the decisions of our leaders. We emphasized that only Heavenly Father knew if my heart was totally right. Only He could judge whether it was time for me to come back into the Church. We explained to the children that God would inspire the Stake President to make the right decision, and we must be prepared to accept a "no" if that was his feeling. We agreed that as much as we all wanted the baptism, even more than that we must want to be in harmony with God's will. Then we knelt in a circle holding hands, and each took a turn in prayer. The thrust of each prayer was gratitude for my conversion and healing, gratitude for having our family secure in our love, and for the Spirit to inspire the President and move him to the proper decision. There were many silent tears and many audible sobs.

After the prayers, our hearts were warm and confident that God would be a real part of this important interview, just as He had been a part of my healing. What a wonderful bond there was between us as we hugged and kissed each other. What a moving experience it was to hear and feel the intense depth of desire each child expressed to have me back in the Church with them.

This would be my first interview with my Stake President since the original court, but there was no fear in my heart as I approached his home. I felt completely calm and confident. I knew that my old man of sin had been crucified and that I had been made a new creature in Christ through the refining fires of adversity. Even though I had not yet been baptized and pronounced clean, I felt clean because I had a personal witness that I was now acceptable to the Lord. If there were some reason the President felt the need to say "No, not yet," I could accept it, knowing that I was right with God.

I expressed those feelings in my interview. I told him of our family unity and how blessed I felt that my family had stood with me through all the anguish. I told him of my conversion and of the things I had discovered about the gospel. I explained my new understanding of the atonement, which I had taken previously for granted.

At the beginning of the interview, it was obvious that he was very reserved and cautious. He confided to me that he had once allowed the rebaptism of a person too soon and that it had broken his heart to see the transgression repeated with all the resulting penalties and heartaches. His caution was obvious from both his questions and posture. But as the interview progressed, and as the Spirit filled the room, there came a visible point at which he smiled and relaxed. He had received what he needed as my judge—the witness of the Spirit.

Before the Stake President would make any final judgement or commitments, however, he wanted a chance to interview my wife. He felt he could learn much about me from her feelings. Surely, this was a wise decision, but it was hard to endure the waiting as her interview was scheduled a few weeks later. When the time came, she, too, came away from his kind and gentle interview feeling that it had been guided by the Spirit. He would only say to her, as he had said to me, that he would make it a matter of earnest prayer.

Coming back into the Church is not a light matter. It is an extremely important decision because the Lord has warned of even more severe penalties if the transgression is repeated. (See D&C 82:7.) He will not be mocked! I appreciate the caution and care manifest by my Stake President. I went before him prepared to outline my good deeds with a checklist, as it were, of the evidence of my repentance. But his questions and the guidance of the Spirit directed the interview into a careful examination of my heart, my testimony, and my commitments. I came away grateful that it was not an easy interview.

As we waited for his decision, we expressed our gratitude to the Lord for His guidance, and continued our pleas for a positive response. We also prayed for the strength to accept the answer if it should be negative. How excited and thrilled we were to receive the following letter:

Dear Brother Cramer,

It was a special privilege to meet with you and your wife recently to discuss your progress and goals regarding your application for rebaptism into the Church. I am pleased that you are making such excellent progress.

After prayerful consideration of the matter, we have scheduled a high council court to consider your rebaptism for____(date)____in the high council room at 8:00 p.m. We request that you be present. If it is not possible for you to attend at the time and place specified, please let me know, and we will schedule it for another time.

As I have explained to you before, a positive recommendation of the court will consist of a request to the First Presidency for approval of the baptism.[1] The ordinance can be performed only upon their approval. Following the rebaptism and after a period of probation, application must be made to the First Presidency for restoration of your priesthood and temple blessings.

If you concur with the time and place set for the court, please indicate your receipt of this notice and your acceptance of the date by signing the enclosed copy of this letter and returning it to me.

May the Lord continue to bless you in your efforts to accomplish the righteous desires of your heart.

Sincerely,

I have already related the care and cautious concern with which the original court deliberated their verdict. The same care was taken this time. Both my bishop and my wife had been requested to provide the court with written statements of testimony concerning my conversion and their feelings about my possible rebaptism. The following is part of the testimony which my wife provided:

Dear President _____,

In reply to your request that I submit a statement regarding my feelings about my husband's excommunication and possible reacceptance back into the Kingdom, and after a great deal of thought and prayer, I offer the following:

First, I have no doubt that the action of the court was just and in accordance with the Lord's will, nor do I regret the awful scenes of trial and adversity that passed

_____

[1]This is not necessary in all cases.

on our family subsequent to that action.

My husband is a very strong and determined man. He was strong enough to consistently attend Church even during his bitterest trials and he was so determined to make it back (on his own) that it took years of bitter and intense suffering to bring him to his knees in utter hopelessness and to admit to himself and to the Lord that he could not do it by himself. I wish I could adequately describe to you the awful despair and helplessness he felt at that time. Suffice it to say that he was in hell and could see no way out on his own power.

He reached this rock-bottom plateau last January, and it was at this point that we both, independently and unbeknownst to the other, cried out to the Lord in mighty supplication for His merciful intervention in his behalf. At last we both knew that he would only make it back, if at all, through the help of the Lord, and it was at this point that God began to work a miracle in his life — and consequently in mine and the children's also.

. . . I felt so strongly that it was out of my hands now and into the hands of Someone who could really help him . . . I felt as though a huge load had been removed from me, and it was as if the Lord said to me, "You've done enough and done it well. Now relax and see My power made manifest in his behalf." The relief was so great that it can't be described. There is no question but that the Lord guided us into this solution step by step. I know He took over to provide the way for my husband's escape from sin and the clutches of Satan. How great and marvelous and merciful is God!

By the end of June, Steven was undeniably a changed man. This change was reflected in every aspect of his life, but I noticed it particularly in our marriage relationship and in his relationships with our children. It was such an amazing change that it took me several months to comprehend that it was real and honest. Now I truly understand that when the Lord affects a healing, He heals the *whole* man from the inside out.

I am experiencing for the first time the love of a man rich in kindness, tolerance and compassion; a man who truly loves the Lord and can feel and express gratitude. He has become a man who lets wisdom rule his interaction with his children and not temper nor intolerance. He has become, at last, the head of our family and has in every way justified our faith in him and earned our respect and love.

Whether or not the time is right for his rebaptism and acceptance into the Church, he is right with the Lord and we, his wife and children, are content to follow him and support him as we wait in patience for that time to arrive.

Sincerely yours,

After the minutes of the original court were reviewed along with this letter and my Bishop's letter, the President expressed his feelings about his interview with my wife and myself. Then it was time for me to speak on my own behalf. This was much more difficult than I had expected it to be. I felt a powerful presence of the Lord's Spirit in the room. I felt the combined strength and love of those sixteen brethren, and I felt such an overwhelming gratitude to God for bringing me to this point that I could hardly speak. My testimony was frequently interrupted by uncontrollable weeping, but this time they were tears of gratitude instead of the bitter tears of remorse that I had shed at the first court. I expressed the feelings that were in my heart for the Lord and His Church and for my family. When the testimonies and questions were completed, I was excused; and the court counselled together to receive the Lord's will concerning me. Twenty-five minutes later, they called me back to give me the joyous verdict: they felt a unanimous agreement to recommend me for rebaptism. We received the following letter shortly thereafter:

Dear Brother Cramer,

This is to formally notify you of the results of the high council court held in your behalf on this date. Since you were present, you are already aware that it was the decision of the court that we recommend to the First Presidency that approval be granted for your rebaptism.[2]

---

[2]Such approval is not necessary in all cases.

We rejoice with you over this decision and are grateful for your courage and determination to overcome the problems that have confronted you. We recognize also that the love and support of a good wife and fine children have assisted you in your accomplishment.

We will transmit the results of the court to the First Presidency and await their decision before the baptism can actually be performed.

May the Lord bless you in your future endeavors.

Sincerely,

How we rejoiced to receive those beautiful words. How can I describe the feeling of relief and gratitude of having those brethren give official ratification to my personal feelings of repentance? What a wonderful blessing God has given us to provide the formal ecclesiastical procedure of the Church to examine and ratify the changes which take place in our lives as we finally make our life right with the Lord.

Many months before this, I had posted 3 × 5 cards in my bedroom, den, and bathroom saying simply, "I AM GOING TO MAKE IT." Now, without announcement or ceremony, the children quietly crossed all the middle words out and wrote above them the word, "MADE" so that the card read, "I MADE IT!" I can imagine their joy in making that change.

Because I was working nights, I usually got up between 9:00 and 10:00 p.m. to say goodnight to the family, eat supper, and prepare for work. I will always remember that special evening about a month later when I got up as usual, but as soon as I sat down to eat, the family came one by one to kiss and hug me, saying, "Congratulations, Dad." With each child I grew more and more curious, and then they told me the good news—the sacred and wonderful news. Our Bishop had called during the day to say that permission had been granted for my rebaptism. It was almost more than I could believe. What a privilege and honor to become a member of God's divine Kingdom! How earnestly I have prayed that I would never again jeopardize that membership or offend God by deliberate sin.

It didn't take long to make the arrangements. Friends and relatives dropped what they were doing and came to share our joy only four days later. When I was placed under the water, my impression was one of literally being buried, and it felt so good, knowing what was being buried there, that I wanted my body to just keep going down, down deeper and deeper, placing my old man of sin forever beyond reach or view. All too soon I was lifted back in symbolism of the new birth which Christ had given me. That newness of life, that wonderful feeling of being whole and complete before Him, erases the awful memories of the past, making it possible to open our hearts to His infinite love. Far more than a symbol, baptism is truly the doorway to a new life.

Following my baptism, I was allowed to participate in church functions the same as any new member who did not hold the priesthood. It was a great step forward to be a small part of the Church and to have the sacred privilege of serving the Master, even in a limited capacity.

After a lengthy period of probation which was measured in years, not weeks or months, my request for the restoration of my priesthood and temple blessings was approved by the prophet, and I was granted an interview with a General Authority who came to our city for a Stake Conference. After his careful and lengthy interview, he placed his hands upon my head. He pronounced me clean and restored each priesthood and temple blessing individually. What an incredible thrill we experienced as my wife and I embraced following that beautiful ordinance. At last we belonged to each other once again, forever!

Later, as I once again reverently placed the holy garment upon my body, it felt as though the Lord, Himself, were there putting His loving arms around me. I felt so safe, so secure, so protected and accepted. It was a witness to me of the power of the temple ordinances.

That same week my wife and I went through the temple together for the first time in many years. What words can describe the feelings of being whole, of being complete, of belonging and knowing that you are accepted? I can only say that it is worth any sacrifice that is required.

As quickly as possible we obtained temple recommends for each of our children who had been baptized. Then, except for our eldest son who was away at school, the whole family went to the temple to have our little daughter, who had been born during the time I was excommunicated, sealed to us. It was a truly inspiring experience to have our children surround us in the temple, each one dressed in white, looking like a small company of angels. As my wife and I knelt at the altar, our little girl beside us with her tiny hand on ours, we received the precious sealing that made our family complete eternally.

Following that ordinance, we all stood where the children could see their image reflected endlessly in the mirrors, and each one promised to live worthy to come back to the temple for their own marriages.

As enormously rewarding and satisfying as these experiences were to me, the major emotion that I felt was a tremendous sense of gratitude for having given back to my family that which I had so cruelly taken from them so many years before. Yet, what we have now is infinitely better than what we had before. Now it is real and eternal and truly appreciated.

EPILOGUE
There Is Always A Way Back

I HAVE COMPLETED my story. I have bared my soul. I have confessed the wickedness of my past. I have shared some of the sacred experiences which brought me to the Lord. There is one more thing to do and that is to express my total assurance that no matter who you are, no matter what you have done (or are still doing), the Lord loves you! He wants you! He is waiting for you as He waited for me. He knows the way back for you. He already has your rescue planned. He is only waiting for you to come to Him. Satan would have us believe that we have gone too far, that it is "too late." That is a lie. It is never too late to turn back.

Something happened to the Prophet Jeremiah that is important to every excommunicant who is struggling to find victory over the faults and failures in his life. Jeremiah tells us that the word of the Lord came to him saying, "Arise, and go down to the potter's house, and there I will cause thee to hear my words." (Jer. 18:2.) We may be sure that Jeremiah's curiosity was aroused by this strange instruction. Certainly, he was used to communing with the Lord on isolated mountain peaks, in the privacy of the forests, perhaps even in the barren wilderness, but why in a cluttered, dusty potter's shop?

Jeremiah tells us that when he arrived, the potter was busy at his trade, "and, behold, he wrought [made] a work

on the wheels." (Jer. 18:3.) As Jeremiah watched him form
the clay into a beautiful vessel on the flat spinning wheel,
something quite natural happened which the Lord knew was
going to happen.

> And the vessel that he made of clay was marred in
> the hand of the potter: so he made it again another
> vessel, as seemed good to the potter to make it. (Jer.
> 18:4.)

As Jeremiah watched the potter's careful work develop
a flaw that made the vessel unacceptable and unusable, he
must have sensed the potter's disappointment. The vessel was
ruined, after all that work. But, to Jeremiah's surprise, the
potter did not discard the broken vessel for a new lump of
clay. Patiently, the potter crushed the vessel back into a
lump of clay. After carefully kneading it, he put the very
same clay back on the spinning wheel and began all over
again to refashion the clay that had been "marred" into the
vessel he had in mind for it all along. There was no anger.
The marred clay was not cast aside for a new lump. The
potter simply accepted the flaw that appeared as a natural
part of life and patiently began again to achieve his
objective. As Jeremiah watched this happen, as he witnessed
this wonderful demonstration of tolerance, patience, and
even forgiveness, the word of the Lord came to him again,
saying:

> O house of Israel, cannot I do with you as this
> potter? saith the Lord. Behold, as the clay is in the
> potter's hand, so are ye in mine hand, O house of
> Israel. (Jer. 18:6.)

And then Jeremiah, who had suffered so much
disappointment and frustration over Israel's stubborn
refusal to submit their lives to the will of the great Jehovah,
suddenly understood. Israel's apostasy and sin could not
discourage the Lord! God's love for us is stronger than our
sin! Nothing we do can cause Him to reject us. No matter
how great our flaw, no matter how many times He has to
forgive and start over, God is going to persist in His love and

patience towards us until all who will respond to Him are able to live the commandments and become the people, the very Zion He is trying to establish.

Now Jeremiah began to comprehend the reality of God's amazing forgiveness and patience with a faltering Israel because he finally understood that God sees our flaws as temporary problems, as opportunities for us to grow and become better. Now Jeremiah understood the wonderful truth that God will always see past our sins and weaknesses to our divine potential. He knows that everyone of us can achieve this if we will only yield ourselves to His will, like clay in the potter's hand, and follow the commandments.

Some of us have more serious "flaws" than others. Some have transgressed so deeply that, for a time, they must be cut off from the Church. But, as Jeremiah learned, now we can know that no flaw, no failure or problem in our life, not even excommunication, can change God's love for us. Perhaps, for a time, the excommunicant's heart has grown cold and hard and refuses to be shaped by the Lord. That is why excommunication is so painful, because we are resisting God's will for us and trying to "fashion" our own vessel.

The time can come, it will come, when the buffetings of Satan and the sorrows suffered from excommunication will wear away the anger and hurt and pride which are keeping us from peace and victory. Then, when the heart finally breaks in humility, when our hearts are soft and our spirits are contrite, God will begin to fashion in us "again another vessel, as seeme[th] good to the [Master] to make it." Jeremiah learned that man may give up on God, but God never gives up on man. There is hope for every person. How wonderful this knowledge is!

It does not matter how long our sorrows have weighed us down; it does not matter how deep our transgressions are; it does not matter how deep our despair is; if we will humbly and sincerely come to the Lord in a repentant attitude and allow Him to be in charge of our life, there is hope. It may be true that we feel totally lost and helpless. Our enemy, Satan, would have us believe that such feelings are permanent, but no one, other than Sons of Perdition, is beyond the Lord's help. Outside this small, defiant group, no one is beyond the power and grace of the Lord.

> Wherefore he is able also to save them to the uttermost that come unto God by him . . . (Heb. 7:25.)

To the uttermost! How beautiful those words are. Jesus Christ really did come into this world to save people from their problems. No one is beyond His love and help. To the uttermost! Oh, what hope this should give us. He sees within every person a soul of inestimable worth. Within every person He sees the soul which can obtain the victory. When He said, "I am able to make you holy . . ." (D&C 60:7), He was telling us that He knows how to help us discard the outward man of sin and weakness and He knows how to give birth to the real person hidden within. Whatever you have allowed to hold you back, let go of it now. Cast it aside for the treasure that can be yours through the miracle of the Savior's infinite power, love, and atonement. It is never too late.

When a person's legs are hopelessly infected with gangrene, and amputation is required, the surgery should not be viewed as negative but as positive. Why? Because it is the only chance left for the individual to continue a healthy life. And so it is with the spiritual life of the excommunicant. If the spiritual fault in his life was so minor that it only required a Band-aid, the Lord would not have required the major surgery of excommunication. But, unlike amputation, excommunication can be reversed and totally erradicated from one's life. It need not be permanent.

The greatest need of the excommunicant is to purge himself of everything in his life that is filthy, wicked, and offensive to the Lord, and to fill his life with true spirituality in the pattern of the Savior. But the excommunicant does not know how to do this nor does he possess the power to work this miracle of rebirth within himself any more than the "marred" vessel of clay could refashion itself. What the excommunicant really needs, then, is a working relationship with the Master Potter, our Savior, Jesus Christ, so that He may supply this crucial need.

Paul promised that God wants to work with us and supply our needs "exceeding abundantly above all that we ask or think" and "according to the power that worketh in us." (Eph. 3:20. See also Philip. 4:19.) What is the power that is working inside the excommunicant? It may be the power of Satan, the individual's own power, or the power of the Lord. No mortal has the power within himself to save himself. We all need to draw upon the power of Jesus Christ if we hope to ever become like Him. If the excommunicated person refuses to "lean on the Lord" and insists on relying on nothing but his own power and wisdom, he is trying to "fashion" his own vessel and is shutting the Lord out of his life. But when he finally admits his need, and surrenders his life to the Savior, and yields himself as submissively as the clay, only then can the Savior intervene in his life and effect the spiritual healing that must occur before rebaptism is even a possibility. Is it any wonder that faith in Jesus Christ is the first principle of the gospel?

God does not expect anyone to find his way to perfection all by himself. When asked how we can find our way to the Father, the Savior said, "I am the way . . . no man cometh unto the Father but by me." (John 14:6.) *He has never asked anyone to walk that path alone, not even the excommunicant.* The Savior promised that He would send the Holy Ghost to "reprove [or convince] the world of sin . . ." (John 16:8.) The excommunicant has forfeited his right to the companionship of the Holy Ghost, but the Lord will work with him to correct his flaws, and He will allow the Holy Ghost to "reprove" and quicken the individual's conscience from time to time as He brings to the excommunicant an awareness, step by step, of the next area that he needs to correct. Obtaining that inspiration is very difficult, for Satan will do everything within his awful power to prevent it. Even though it comes at a high price, it can be found. God is only waiting for that happy time when the excommunicant's heart is truly ready to receive.

The following quotations and scriptures provide sacred assurance that there is a way back for every person. Study them carefully, for they testify that there is always a way back, even "to the uttermost," through the power of repentance and Christ's redeeming love.

> And we know that all things [even an excommunication] work together for good to them that love God . . . (Rom. 8:28.)

> Even excommunication from the Church need not be the end of all hope. Although the mistake has been a grievous and serious violation of God's commandments, a person who really loves the Lord and has the desire and the fortitude to submit himself to priesthood authority can re-establish his life and in due process qualify himself for the lofty and ultimate blessings of eternity, including exaltation. *Even the gross offender will be welcomed back by the Lord:* "Though your sins be as scarlet, they shall be white as snow." (Isa. 1:18.) What a great promise, what a great redemption! (Robert L. Simpson, *The New Era,* Jan. 1977, p. 7; emphasis added.)

> Thus we may see that the Lord is merciful unto all who will, in the sincerity of their hearts, call upon his holy name.

> Yea, thus we see that *the gate of heaven is open unto all,* even to those who will believe on the name of Jesus Christ, who is the Son of God. (Hel. 3:27-28; emphasis added.)

> Behold, he sendeth an invitation unto all men, for the arms of mercy are extended towards them, and he saith: *Repent, and I will receive you.* (Alma 5:33; emphasis added.)

> For we have not an high priest which cannot be touched with the feeling of our infirmities; *but was in all points tempted like as we are,* yet without sin.

*Let us therefore come boldly unto the throne of
grace, that we may obtain mercy, and find grace to help
in time of need.* (Heb. 4:15-16; emphasis added.)

We think we must climb to a certain height of
goodness before we can reach God. But He says not "at
the end of the way you may find me;" He says, "I am
the way; I am the road under your feet, the road that
begins just as low down as you happen to be."
If we are in a hole then the Way begins in the hole.
The moment we set our face in the same direction as
His, we are walking with God. (Helen Wodehouse, as
quoted in *Prayer Can Change Your Life,* William R.
Parker and Elaine St. Johns, 17th Ed., Englewood
Cliffs, N.J.: Prentice-Hall, Inc., 1965, pp. 244-245;
emphasis added.)

. . . he has all power to save every man that believeth on his name and bringeth forth fruit meet for repentance. (Alma 12:15.)

The Lord knoweth how to deliver the godly out of
temptations . . . (2 Pet. 2:9.)

And now, my sons, remember, remember that it is
upon the rock of our Redeemer, who is Christ, the Son
of God, that ye must build your foundation; that when
the devil shall send forth his mighty winds, yea, his
shafts in the whirlwind, yea, when all his hail and his
mighty storm shall beat upon you, *it shall have no
power over you to drag you down to the gulf of misery
and endless wo,* because of the rock upon which ye are
built, which is a sure foundation, *a foundation whereon
if men build they cannot fall.* (Hel. 5:12; emphasis
added.)

On those days when earthly friends may disappoint
you, remember that the Savior of all mankind has described himself as your friend. *He is your very best
friend!* (Spencer W. Kimball, *The New Era,* July 1980,
p. 10; emphasis added.)

Be faithful and diligent in keeping the commandments of God, and I will encircle thee in the arms of my
love. (D&C 6:20.)

APPENDIX A
How Long Does It Take?

REPENTANCE TAKES TIME. All change and improvement take time. Establishing new habits takes time. Finding forgiveness requires time, often a considerable amount of time. There are no short-cuts on the pathway back from sin. The truly repentant person will focus his attention on the repentance rather than the length of time. If one's heart is in the right place, the time will take care of itself. If one is preoccupied with how quickly penalties are to be removed, if his heart is all tangled up in how quickly he can rush through the probation, he will be easily distracted from the changes which must take place before it is appropriate to remove the penalties.

President Kimball has stated that "forgiveness is not a thing of days or months or even years, but is a matter of intensity of feeling and transformation of self." (*The Miracle of Forgiveness*, Salt Lake City, Utah: Bookcraft, Inc., 1969, p. 156.) And yet, he also said that "repentance is inseparable from time." What does this mean? He explains:

> Repentance is inseparable from time. No one can repent on the cross, nor in prison, nor in custody. *One must have the opportunity [time span] of commiting wrong in order to be really repentant.* The man in handcuffs, the prisoner in the penitentiary, the man as he drowns, or as he dies—such a man certainly cannot

repent totally. He can wish to do it, he may intend to change his life, he may determine that he will, but that is only the beginning. (Ibid., pp. 167-168; emphasis added.)

Most people take their sins too lightly. In these days of "instant" everything we too often expect to dismiss our sins with a quick sigh of remorse as we rush on to the next experience. President Kimball has warned that many people "have no conception of satisfying the Lord, of paying the total penalties and obtaining a release and adjustment which could be considered final and which might be accepted of the Lord." (Ibid., p. 156.)

Your Heavenly Father has promised forgiveness upon total repentance and meeting all the requirements, but that forgiveness is not granted merely for the asking. There must be works—many works—and an all-out, total surrender, with a great humility and "a broken heart and a contrite spirit."

It depends upon you whether or not you are forgiven, and when. It could be weeks, it could be years, it could be centuries before that happy day when you have the positive assurance that the Lord has forgiven you. That depends on your humility, your sincerity, your works, your attitudes. (Ibid., pp. 324-325; emphasis added.)

There is a possibility of an excommunicant returning to the blessings of the Church with full membership, and this can only be done through baptism following satisfactory repentance. The way is hard and rough and, without the help of the Holy Ghost to whisper and plead and warn and encourage, one's climb is infinitely harder than if he were to repent before he loses the Holy Ghost, his membership, and the fellowship of the saints. *The time is usually long, very long, as those who have fought their way back will attest.* Any who have been finally restored would give the same advice: Repent first—do not permit yourself to be excommunicated if there is a possible way to save yourself from that dire calamity. (Ibid., pp. 329-330; emphasis added.)

How do we judge when repentance has done its total

work? How do we know when sufficient time has passed? When can we say that new habits and commitments are truly permanent? The 1978-79 Melchizedek Priesthood Manual asks, "When excommunication has occurred by court action, how much time is required before the individual can be readmitted to fellowship in the Church?" In answer, the lesson quotes the following words of Stephen L. Richards from the April 1954 Conference Report, p. 12:

> Surely this determination must rest with the inspired discernment and discretion of the judges. *No specification of time can be definitely made,* but one caution may be wisely observed. That caution is for a sufficient time to elapse to permit a period of probation for the one seeking forgiveness. This probation serves a double purpose: First, and perhaps most important, it enables the offender to determine for himself whether he has been able to so master himself as to trust himself in the face of ever-recurring temptation; and secondly, to enable the judges to make a more reliable appraisement of the genuineness of repentance and worthiness for restored confidence. (p. 177-178; emphasis added.)

The principle involved with repentance and time, then, is that it is far better to be safe than sorry. How unfortunate it would be to waive penalties prematurely and then have the person fall back to the former sins. Such a disaster is devastating to the morale of the individual and makes another repentance and forgiveness infinitely more difficult to obtain.

> . . . unto that soul who sinneth shall the former sins return, saith the Lord your God. (D&C 82:7.)

> Even the Lord will not forgive a person in his sins. If the bishop or stake president is careless and grants forgiveness when it is not justified, the responsibility is with him. (*The Miracle of Forgiveness,* Salt Lake City, Utah: Bookcraft, Inc., 1969, p. 337.)

In the following words, President Kimball makes it clear that the deciding factor in ending an excommunication is not the elapsed time, but "the feel" which Priesthood leaders obtain by inspiration from Heavenly Father and the Savior who await the return of the excommunicant with more intensity of desire than we can know. Because the Church is guided by revelation, when the proper time comes for rebaptism to occur, the same inspiration which was there to initiate the penalty will be there to remove it.

The rules concerning the handling of these matters are somewhat flexible. Recognizing that repentance is vital to the salvation of all of us since all men sin in a lesser or a greater degree, and since *the intensity of repentance, which is an intangible thing, can be determined fully only by inspiration and discernment,* it is left generally to the discretion of the ecclesiastical leader to decide on the treatment of the case, since all cases are different. Some are vicious, intentional, premeditated, repeated and unrepented of; others seem to have some extenuating circumstances or may have been done under a moment of passion or pressures of unusual situations, and are followed by sincere repentance. Accordingly, the treatment of these cases is left largely to the bishop in the ward or the president in the stake or the president of the mission.

In my experience, I have found repentance is also an intangible. *One must judge by the feel rather than by what is said or done,* and in my experience, numerous times two people have committed the same sin and one might be eligible for forgiveness and the blessings of the Church in months where another would not be ready in years. In fact, I have seen this — one hard and cold and belligerent and unrepentant, and the other bowed in "sackcloth and ashes" with a "broken heart and a contrite spirit" and willing to do anything to make good. *It must be obvious that no period of one year or ten years or one month or a lifetime should be the determining factor.* (Ibid., pp. 336-337; emphasis added.)

APPENDIX B
Recommended Reading

BECAUSE I RECEIVED so much help from the following books, I am recommending them to the reader for the reasons stated.

1. *The Miracle of Forgiveness,* Spencer W. Kimball, Salt Lake City, Utah: Bookcraft, Inc.

This book should be read and studied repeatedly. Each time it is read, the Spirit will open one's understanding to new and important truths. I know of no other book which can contribute more to the excommunicant's understanding of the gravity of his sin, why he is suffering, and the pathway back to forgiveness and peace.

2. *Drawing on the Powers of Heaven,* Grant Von Harrison, Provo, Utah: The Ensign Publishing Company

This short book is excellent for learning the principles and practical procedures involved in making one's faith and prayer effective.

3. *In His Footsteps Today,* 1969-70 Gospel Doctrine Manual, Salt Lake City, Utah: Deseret Sunday School Union

This manual really helped me to discover the power of character and habit control to be gained by analyzing my day-to-day choices in terms of, "What would Jesus do?" This manual presents ideas and insights which opened my awareness to my need for a personal relationship with the Savior. It helped me to learn that the closer I emulate the Savior, the better I know Him and the closer I feel to Him.

4. *Gifts of the Spirit,* Duane S. Crowther, Salt Lake City, Utah: Bookcraft, Inc.

This is one of the finest books available on learning to appreciate the ministry of the Holy Spirit, and how to accept the benefits of increased spirituality in our lives.

5. *Developing A Personal Relationship With the Savior,* George W. Pace, Tape Cassette Recording, Salt Lake City, Utah: Covenant Recordings, Inc., 1979

This is the Tape Recording which the Spirit used to teach me of my need for spiritual healing through the power of the atonement of Christ. The talk pierced the darkness of forty years of spiritual blindness and showed me the futility of trying to substitute behavioral modification for the real change in human nature which can only come through Jesus Christ.

6. "Courts of Love," Robert L. Simpson, *Ensign,* July 1972, pp. 48-49

"Cast Your Burden Upon the Lord," Robert L. Simpson, *New Era,* January 1977, pp. 4-8

No examination of excommunication could be considered complete without including these two talks. Both are classics; they represent the finest commentaries available. Every priesthood leader, every family, and every individual who is in any way connected to the process of an excommunication or disfellowshipment should be completely familiar with the information and the spirit which these two talks present.

7. *Prayer Can Change Your Life,* William R. Parker & Elaine St. Johns, Englewood Cliffs, New Jersey: Prentice-Hall, Inc.

This book was written by a psychologist who was unable to cope with the guilt and stress in his own life in spite of all his psychological wisdom. When he found peace and spiritual healing through prayer, he dedicated his life to the analysis and discovery of why some prayers are effective and others are useless. The principles of prayer which he presents (in easy layman's language) were very inspiring to me. This book helped me to increase my faith in prayer and in God. It also made me aware of Satan's influence against my faith and prayers in ways I had never understood.

8. *Happiness Is A Choice,* (A Manual on the Symptoms, Causes, and Cures of Depression), Frank B. Minirth, M.D., and Paul D. Meier, M.D., Grand Rapids, Mich., Baker Book House.

One might call this a self-treatment book. It was written by two Christian psychologists. They discuss (in layman's language) how Satan uses feelings of discouragement, depression, guilt, helplessness, hopelessness, and worthlessness to defeat us. They also teach how we can draw on God's power to overcome these negative influences and find peace and happiness in Christ.

9. *Mere Christianity,* C. S. Lewis, New York, New York: MacMillan Publishing Co., Inc.

This book might be described as a philosophical defense of Christianity. It gave me many new insights as to how and why gospel principles change lives. It helped me to understand the partnership between God and man in striving towards perfection. It also helped me to discover that I could never become perfect without the help of God, and that with Him as a real part of my life I could never again desire or accept mediocrity, slothfulness, and excuses. This book helped me to understand the relationship of grace and works in a practical way that changed my life and brought me closer to the Savior.

The last three books are by non-LDS authors and can be found in almost any library or Christian bookstore.

10. "To Forgive Is Divine," Theodore M. Burton, *Ensign,* May 1983, pp. 70-72.

This challenging talk emphasizes the importance of mercy and forgiveness in the rehabilitation of the excommunicant.